M000093884

Easy Cooking for Two

EASY cooking for two

75 Perfectly Portioned Recipes

Jenna Braddock

MSH, RDN, CSSD

Photography by Hélène Dujardin

ROCKRIDGE
PRESS

Copyright © 2021 by Rockridge Press, Emeryville, California

No part of this publication may be reproduced, stored in a retrieval system, or transmitted in any form or by any means, electronic, mechanical, photocopying, recording, scanning, or otherwise, except as permitted under Sections 107 or 108 of the 1976 United States Copyright Act, without the prior written permission of the Publisher. Requests to the Publisher for permission should be addressed to the Permissions Department, Rockridge Press, 6005 Shellmound Street, Suite 175, Emeryville, CA 94608.

Limit of Liability/Disclaimer of Warranty: The Publisher and the author make no representations or warranties with respect to the accuracy or completeness of the contents of this work and specifically disclaim all warranties, including without limitation warranties of fitness for a particular purpose. No warranty may be created or extended by sales or promotional materials. The advice and strategies contained herein may not be suitable for every situation. This work is sold with the understanding that the Publisher is not engaged in rendering medical, legal, or other professional advice or services. If professional assistance is required, the services of a competent professional person should be sought. Neither the Publisher nor the author shall be liable for damages arising herefrom. The fact that an individual, organization, or website is referred to in this work as a citation and/or potential source of further information does not mean that the author or the Publisher endorses the information the individual, organization, or website may provide or recommendations they/it may make. Further, readers should be aware that websites listed in this work may have changed or disappeared between when this work was written and when it is read.

For general information on our other products and services or to obtain technical support, please contact our Customer Care Department within the United States at (866) 744-2665, or outside the United States at (510) 253-0500.

Rockridge Press publishes its books in a variety of electronic and print formats. Some content that appears in print may not be available in electronic books, and vice versa.

TRADEMARKS: Rockridge Press and the Rockridge Press logo are trademarks or registered trademarks of Callisto Media Inc. and/or its affiliates, in the United States and other countries, and may not be used without written permission. All other trademarks are the property of their respective owners. Rockridge Press is not associated with any product or vendor mentioned in this book.

Interior and Cover Designer: Jami Spittler
Art Producer: Sue Bischofberger
Editor: Rachelle Cihonski
Production Editor: Ashley Polikoff

Photography © 2021 Hélène Dujardin; food styling by Anna Simpson

Author photo courtesy of Michelle VanTine Photography

ISBN: Print 978-1-64876-032-7 | eBook 978-1-64876-033-4

R0

For those in pursuit of
a more vibrant life through
delicious and easy food.

Contents

Introduction

In the mid-2000s, I was a young newlywed and a registered dietitian. I was bound and determined to make delicious but easy and balanced meals for my husband and myself. Unfortunately, it was a struggle to find delicious, easy recipes that made just enough food for two people. I hate to admit that in those early years I wasted a lot of food testing alternatives to big-batch recipes or simply having way too many leftovers.

This cookbook is for anyone in similar circumstances. Whether you're a newlywed, an empty nester, a single parent of one child, newly coupled, or living with a roommate, I hope this book becomes your go-to guide for getting quick and delicious meals on your table while also minimizing food waste.

While I was writing these recipes, one of my neighbors became my trusted taste-tester. Her feedback was so helpful, and I knew I had the perfect recipe when she told me, "I'd make this." As you flip through these pages of recipes, I hope you will say the same thing.

Every recipe in this book was created to whet your appetite and spark confidence in the kitchen, all while delivering easy options. My hope is that you'll never dread the question, "What should I cook?" You'll simply pick up this book for the answer.

Grocery List

- Carrots
- Lemons
- Potatoes
- Apples
- Milk
- Butter
- Beans
- Mushrooms
- Asparagus
- Rice

- Avocados
- Red wine
- olive oil

Chapter 1

Making Easy
Meals for Two

We are creatures of habit, and when it comes to grocery shopping, cooking, and eating, that fact couldn't be more apparent. It's easy to engage autopilot and grocery shop the way you always have or how you saw your parents do it. You wander down the same aisles and buy the same things. Meals become monotonous, and you can't remember the last time you made something new and interesting.

There could be several reasons you're reading this book on cooking for two. Perhaps you were single but have found that special someone. Maybe you gained a roommate. Possibly you're cooking for yourself and sick of eating leftovers for four days. Or you spent years cooking for a crowd, but the kids have grown up and moved out. Perhaps a leaner budget or even your conscience has led you to confront your food waste, and you need a gentle nudge in the right direction.

Whatever circumstances have brought you here, I'm so happy to share this collection of delicious, easy recipes perfectly portioned for two. They are designed to be your go-to arsenal for busy days: simple to shop for, prep, and execute. The finished dishes also taste delicious.

Cooking Perfectly Portioned Meals

Finding recipes that yield only two portions might feel like searching for the Holy Grail of menu planning. Two-portion recipes are scarce, and larger portions require serious math skills for dividing ingredient measurements in half (or more). You can breathe a sigh of relief, because this book has done all the hard work for you. Every recipe is designed to feed only two. This streamlined approach to cooking has numerous benefits, including:

▹ **MINIMIZING FOOD WASTE** — Conserving food is one of the most impactful ways to help the environment.

▹ **NO LEFTOVER BURNOUT** — Who wants to eat the same thing for days and days?

▹ **SMALLER GROCERY BILLS** — You'll learn the tricks for buying only what you need.

▹ **LESS TIME IN THE KITCHEN** — You'll be cooking less food and cleaning fewer dishes.

▹ **LESS RISK** — You can try new foods or cuisines without spending much money because you're making a small amount.

▹ **MINIMAL MATH** — Doubling a recipe to make more than two portions is easier than splitting a recipe for four.

In order to adjust to cooking for two, I recommend developing a few helpful skills:

1. **PLAN MEALS PRIOR TO FOOD SHOPPING.** Sure, it's nice to wander into the grocery store and see what's on sale or what catches your eye, but you'll probably end up buying more than you actually need or will use. Instead, use this book to plan your meals for the week and make a grocery list. A little planning will save you a lot of time and money and also cut down on food waste.

2. **THINK OUTSIDE THE BOX.** Many foods are sold in quantities that are better suited for larger groups of people, like packages of meat, frozen meals, boxed rice or pasta sides, bread, and even fresh produce. This book explains the best way to buy foods that better suit your kitchen for two.

3. **BUILD AN AWARENESS AROUND FOOD WASTE.** Awareness is a critical foundation for any healthy kitchen. According to SaveTheFood.com, 40 percent of all food in America is thrown away. This collective habit has a tremendous impact on the environment, as resources are lost and landfills get, well, fuller. Wasting less food during any part of the process (whether buying, prepping, cooking, storing, or throwing away) is important and impactful.

Easy, Not Boring

One of the hard lessons I've learned from cooking for two is that just because a recipe is easy to make doesn't mean everyone will enjoy it. For a meal to be a viable option in my home, it has to taste good. This cookbook exists to solve this dilemma. Here you will find flavorful meals that are fairly quick to execute. I've also been mindful about keeping cooking vessels to a minimum. (Imagine us high-fiving right now or doing a happy dance because it *is* possible!)

I'm a self-defined "open eater" who enjoys different styles of eating, so this book contains something for everyone. You'll find a variety of recipes, including those that are gluten-free, gluten-full, dairy-free, vegan, vegetarian, and plant and animal protein based. No matter what your tastes or requirements, you will certainly find something to help you broaden your horizons.

Although the main focus of this book is ease, I also created the recipes with balance in mind. As a registered dietitian, I am familiar with the misconception that healthier food is more complicated to prepare. This belief couldn't be further from the truth, and these recipes will prove it. This book takes a simple, stripped-down approach to creating easy, balanced meals.

Shopping for Two

Grocery shopping for two people is different from shopping for a crowd. It takes forethought and often restraint to stick to what you and another person will actually eat.

For whatever reason you find yourself here, understand that shopping for two takes a different mindset. When shopping, asking the following questions can help guide better decision-making:

▷ Is this sale item really a good deal? Will having more of this food benefit me immediately or later?

▷ Do I have time to prepare this food today or tomorrow so I will actually eat it?

▷ If I buy this food, will I have to forgo purchasing something else because of budget constraints, storage space, or time availability?

▷ Is this food available in a different format or packaging that better suits my two-portion needs?

Now, let's break down the sections of the grocery store and equip you with tactics to shop for two with confidence.

Meat and Seafood

When shopping for meat and seafood, it's helpful to think outside the package. Just because meat is displayed a certain way or in a certain quantity does not mean you have to purchase it in that manner. Use the tricks that follow to get the exact amount you want and need when shopping for poultry, red meat, pork, or seafood.

GO BACK TO THE BUTCHER'S COUNTER. Many grocery store meat counters will gladly repackage fresh meat into a different amount or weight than displayed. For example, if fresh steaks are displayed only in three-packs but you need only two, ask the butcher to separate them out for you.

LOOK FOR FROZEN WHEN FRESH ISN'T AVAILABLE. If you don't have a seafood counter at your grocery store, frozen fish is an excellent option. The fish is flash frozen when very fresh and often vacuum sealed as individual fillets, making it easy to cook only two portions. Similarly, frozen shrimp sold in resealable bags allows you to cook only what you need. The same is applicable for poultry and red meat: look for portions that are frozen individually or as two servings together. You can usually find these portions with certain brands of chicken breasts, tenders, or thighs.

DON'T DISMISS BONE-IN OPTIONS. Often sold in a single larger cut of meat, bone-in poultry breasts and legs are the perfect size for two people to share.

INVEST IN A VACUUM SEALER. This amazing kitchen appliance allows you to take advantage of meat sales by portioning your large purchase into single or double servings and vacuum sealing for freezing up to 6 months.

Produce

Produce is one of the biggest food-waste culprits. It's estimated that the average household throws out 48 percent of their fruits and vegetables, according to SaveTheFood.com. It's completely understandable why this happens. You have good intentions and know you should eat them, so you buy them. Unfortunately, you don't have a plan for how you are actually going to prepare and consume the produce. Here are helpful tips for shopping that, along with the recipes to come, will help you buy what you need, waste less, and actually eat those fruits and vegetables.

PICK UP FROZEN PRODUCE. The frozen produce section has become a land of wonder and awe. There are so many exciting options available to assist you with eating quick, healthy meals. Look for diced vegetables (such as butternut squash used in Spicy Butternut Squash Soup on page 19) and spiralized vegetables (such as zucchini for Easy Meatballs over Zucchini Noodles on page 123). In addition, you can find amazing plant-based protein sources (such as edamame for the Warm Quinoa Salad on page 24) and cooked grains (such as brown rice for Pineapple Chicken on page 86). The best part about frozen produce is that it's okay if you don't use it right away or need only a small portion for a recipe. It will stay safe and sound in your freezer, still fully nutritious, until you are ready to use it.

PRECUT ISN'T CHEATING. The fresh produce section provides many time-saving options that also help you buy the right amount, waste less, consume more, and cook mindful portions. Look for precut melon, onions, peppers, zucchini, and broccoli as well as spiralized vegetables and harder-to-prep vegetables like winter squash. These options are usually sold in package sizes (such as precut watermelon chunks versus a whole melon) that are better suited for a smaller group and therefore prevent waste.

CHOOSE SMALLER ITEMS. Many types of produce are prized for being a certain size or shape that produces uniformity. As a result, you may buy bigger sizes than you actually need. Dig around in the apple, potato, onion, or tomato bins to find the smaller items that better suit your meals for two.

SHOP LOCAL. Farmers' markets are a wonderful option for shopping for two. Many vendors will allow you to buy only the quantity of produce you need. You may find fruit and vegetables in more unique shapes and sizes than you are used to, but this does not mean they taste bad. In fact, they often have surprisingly good flavor!

Grains, Breads, and Dried Goods

With a little creativity, you can easily shop for dry goods for two. You also may find that some stores better accommodate your shopping needs based on these tips.

SHOP BULK SECTION BINS. Many grocery stores now have a bulk food department for beans, nuts, flours, grains, nut butters, spices, and snacks. Although these floor-to-ceiling bins may look intimidating, they allow you to buy only what you need—often at a lower price. You also might find some foods that aren't usually packaged on the shelf, such as short-grain brown rice, a personal favorite.

KNOW YOUR BAKERY. Buying bread products for two can be a drag because you often need less than what is offered. You can freeze bread for later use, but do you want to store half a dozen rolls in your freezer? Instead, get to know the bakery section of your store. Ask what items they can break down into smaller portions. For instance, if you're making Banh Mi–Style Sandwiches (page 96), ask if you can purchase only two rolls. Your local bakery will likely be happy to sell you only the amount you need as well.

TRY FROZEN VERSIONS. Many grains are now available in the frozen food section of your grocery store. They stay fresh longer and give you the freedom to use only what you need. In addition, frozen grains are already cooked and simply need to be heated, which saves time.

MAKE A SPECIFIC SHOPPING LIST. When you need dry goods from the store, instead of just writing "bread" on your list, note what you need it for. Including details such as "sandwiches at lunch" or "for soup night" can help you pick up only what you need for that recipe.

Canned, Jarred, and Bottled Goods

I've met many people who think it's necessary to avoid the center aisles of the grocery store. Although it's true that many whole foods are found around the perimeter, the center aisles contain time-saving, flavor-adding, wholesome foods too. Try these tips for discovering easy-to-use ingredients on your next shopping trip.

CANNED GOODS ARE OKAY. Canned vegetables can be a lifesaver when you need food fast. My favorites are all kinds of beans, every type of canned tomatoes, olives, artichokes, mushrooms, and corn, to name a few. I recommend looking for no- or reduced-sodium options. Two of my secret weapons for flavorful dishes are the tomato paste in a squeezable tube (to add umami flavor) and fire-roasted tomatoes. Keep your pantry stocked with these staples, which are used frequently in these recipes.

BIG FLAVOR COMES IN LITTLE BOTTLES. Using vinegar and wine is an easy way to add big flavor to dishes with little to no effort. You'll see a variety of types used in the recipes in this book. When buying vinegar, look for high-quality brands in smaller bottles. You don't need an enormous bottle when cooking for two, and you'll get better flavor. Purchase wine in single-serving-bottle 4-packs so you always have it on hand and don't waste a whole bottle for a single recipe.

AVOID THE JARRED CONDIMENT GRAVEYARD. I don't know about you, but about once a year I have to do a thorough purging of random leftover condiments at the back of my refrigerator. To prevent this waste, look for condiments in single-serving options. For example, instead of buying a whole jar of pickles, buy a single snacking pickle, often found by the refrigerated pickles or in the snack aisle, and chop it up yourself.

FREEZE TO SAVE. Many condiments or canned goods can be frozen after opening to preserve freshness. You can use an ice-cube tray to form them into perfect single servings. Once frozen, transfer them to a resealable bag, where they're ready to be used at a moment's notice. This practice works well with tomato paste, crushed tomatoes, thicker sauces such as hoisin, lemon or lime juice, and fresh herbs in butter or oil.

Dairy and Nondairy Alternatives

There are so many options for milks, yogurt, and cheese these days that the dairy section can feel overwhelming. Here are some ideas for locating the right quantity for two.

BIGGER IS NOT ALWAYS BETTER. It's tempting to buy the bigger size of dairy products because it's a better value. But if you're not going to be able to consume it before it goes bad, you're actually losing money. Stick to smaller-size products such as single-serving yogurts (for recipes such as Tempeh Salad with Yogurt Basil Dressing on page 25) or quarts of milk instead of gallons.

LOOK FOR SINGLES. Although many single-serving dairy products are marketed for lunchboxes, they're also perfect for a group of two. Check out options such as single-serving cheeses, usually displayed with the shredded cheese or cottage cheese, often next to the yogurt cups. This packaging ensures longer freshness and shelf life.

A Kitchen for Two

You need the right kitchen tools to cook for two. Correct portion sizes look puny in big pans, and it's no fun to clean more (or larger) dishes than needed. Here are my suggestions for the kitchen tools that are just right for two:

SMALL DUTCH OVEN (2½ TO 3½ QUARTS). Dutch ovens are the workhorse of the kitchen. You can cook almost anything in them on the stovetop or in the oven.

SMALL BAKING DISHES (7-BY-5-INCH RECTANGULAR OR 3.1-QUART AU GRATIN). This size is perfect for baking or roasting for two.

HEAVY-DUTY SKILLET (10 TO 12 INCHES). Although smaller skillet sizes exist, I think it's important to have a little space in your pan for even cooking. Cast iron or stainless steel are the most versatile, but choose the material you are most comfortable with.

QUARTER BAKING SHEETS. These rimmed baking sheets are the perfect size for two servings of protein or roasted vegetables. I also like that they are small enough to allow you to fit other things in your oven and are great for pre-freezing items.

DUAL LEAVE-IN DIGITAL MEAT THERMOMETER. This type of digital thermometer tracks two separate probes and lets you know the temperature of two pieces of meat simultaneously. Some will even sound an alarm when meat is cooked thoroughly. You can also use it to take the temperature of meat you cook on the stovetop.

POWERFUL BLENDER OR IMMERSION BLENDER. There is a difference between traditional blenders and high-powered ones. Aside from the big jump in price, powerful blenders always get the job done without leaving chunks or getting jammed. A more economical and space-saving option is a handheld immersion blender that you can stick right in your pot and blend on the spot. This tool saves on dishes and speeds up the blending process.

MEASURING SPOONS AND SILICONE LIQUID MEASURING CUP. The recipes in this book call for fractions of a teaspoon of spices to adjust appropriately for two servings. Make sure you have a good measuring spoon set with

Minimizing Food Waste

There are a lot of ways to help reduce your carbon footprint, and reducing your food waste is a rock-solid way to do your part. Here's how to begin.

1. **SHOP FROM YOUR REFRIGERATOR, FREEZER, AND PANTRY FIRST.** Before going grocery shopping, take inventory of your own supply and see if you can make any meals from the food you already have. Many recipes in this book use pantry ingredients.

2. **BUY IT ONLY IF YOU'LL EAT IT.** It's very tempting to buy what's on sale simply because it's marked down or seems like a better value. But if you're not going to consume the food, it's just a waste.

3. **PREP PRODUCE AS SOON AS YOU GET HOME FROM THE STORE.** Wash and cut vegetables right away. You'll be far more likely to eat them if you've already done the work.

INGREDIENTS	MONDAY	TUESDAY
KALE, YOGURT, AND SLAW	Avocado-Kale Salad with Seared Salmon (page 27)	Mahi Sandwich with Tangy Slaw (page 67)
SALSA VERDE, PEPPERS, AND BRUSSELS SPROUTS	Black Bean–Stuffed Bell Peppers with Plantains (page 39)	Bacon, Brussels Sprouts, and Egg Bowls (page 110)
GROUND TURKEY, BUTTERNUT SQUASH, AND SPINACH	Buffalo Turkey Meatballs (page 102)	Spicy Butternut Squash Soup (page 19)
COCONUT MILK, CHICKEN THIGHS, AND CABBAGE	Quick Chickpea Curry (page 36)	Quick Weeknight Gumbo (page 100)

4. **GET COMFORTABLE WITH FREEZING.** Freezing leftovers and produce is a fantastic way to keep them out of your trash can. You can easily freeze soup, cooked grains, cooked meat, greens, fruit, and vegetables. Purchase single-serving frost-proof containers for easy defrosting and reheating.

5. **KNOW WHAT THE DATES MEAN.** Many food products are printed with dates so consumers and stores know when food quality is at its peak. The following date descriptions refer to food quality, not food safety: best by, purchase by, best if used before, sell by, use by, and freeze by. Food past these dates is still safe to eat and can be enjoyed instead of thrown out.

In the spirit of minimizing food waste, below are a few quick reference meal plans for using similar ingredients across five days of lunches or dinners.

WEDNESDAY	THURSDAY	FRIDAY
Sweet Potato, Kale, and Egg Stacks (page 46)	Mediterranean-Style Chicken Bowls (page 88)	Beef-Broccoli Stir-Fry (page 124)
Pineapple Chicken (page 86)	Chicken Enchilada Casserole (page 90)	Mom's 10-Minute Salmon with Charred Brussels Sprouts (page 79)
Spinach-Artichoke Pasta (page 50)	Rosemary Turkey Skillet (page 103)	Apricot Chicken with Spinach Rice (page 84)
Chile-Lime Pork Chops with Slaw (page 115)	Mango-Cashew Chicken with Sweet Peas (page 91)	Baked Tilapia Tacos (page 66)

⅛, ¼, and ½ teaspoons. A silicone measuring cup set is a big-time helper in cooking. You can accurately measure (and store) liquids, and it's easier (and neater) to pour from silicone than glass.

VACUUM SEALER. As mentioned on page 5, a vacuum sealer allows you to keep so many foods fresh in your freezer. It also opens up real opportunities for shopping at warehouse stores, where portions are enormous. If something is a good deal but comes in a pack of 10, simply portion it out in pairs at home, vacuum seal it, and store in the freezer.

Recipes for Two

This cookbook is one I was born to write. I love cooking, but the meals I make have to be quick and taste good. Throwing out perfectly good food makes my skin crawl, and most recipes make more food than I need or want.

The recipes in these pages are, first and foremost, fast and delicious. You can also trust that they make just enough food for two. The goal is no leftovers or waste, but you can adjust if you want more or less based on your appetite on a particular night. Each recipe is designed to cover your whole meal. No additional side dishes are needed, but some recipes include suggestions for how to add more to the meal (for example, serving with a simple green salad or crusty bread).

This book does not include dessert recipes, but not because you shouldn't enjoy them. I am a pro-dessert dietitian, but I assume that, like me, you aren't often in the mood to whip up a healthy chocolate cake on a Tuesday night. You also won't find breakfast recipes here because you can typically throw together this meal with no problem. (Hello, scrambled eggs and toast!)

> Yields

All the recipes in this book are complete meals that serve two people, with no intended leftovers. The portion sizes are balanced and fulfilling, and some headnotes include a note for doubling, making a meal more substantial, and storing if you want leftovers.

Familiar Ingredients

Every recipe in this book started with the same bones: fruits or vegetables, protein, carbohydrates containing fiber, and some satisfying fat. Some offer less carbohydrates or a choose-your-own-adventure option with suggestions for easy pairings. Nutrition facts are provided for those who like to know them, and I made every effort to hover these numbers around the Food and Nutrition Board's Recommended Dietary Allowances. My goal is for you to find recipes you enjoy making and eating that provide you great energy and vitality.

You won't have to hunt for exotic or expensive ingredients you use only once. The recipes use a mix of fresh, frozen, and pantry staples throughout, and some offer suggestions for how to use an ingredient in another recipe. A few ingredients might be new to you. Smoked paprika, hoisin sauce, and adobo seasoning, for example, are relied on for their unique flavors and ease of use. I hope you enjoy trying them.

There are two main oils used throughout this book: avocado oil for its healthy fats, mild flavor, and high smoke point, and extra-virgin olive oil for dressings and when flavor matters. Buy these oils in smaller sizes to preserve freshness and avoid taking up too much room in your kitchen. You are also welcome to use the cooking oil you're most comfortable with or need to use up in your pantry.

Tips and Labels

Every recipe includes one of the following tips to give you even more guidance on how to make it, enjoy it differently, or use up an ingredient.

▸ **MAKE IT EASIER** — A tip for making the recipe even easier or quicker with a convenience product or special appliance.

▸ **SWAP OR SUBSTITUTE** — A tip for replacing one ingredient with another in a case of preference or availability.

▸ **USE IT UP** — A tip for using any ingredients in the recipe that may yield leftovers (such as an open can of beans), including any other recipes that call for it.

- **PAIRS WELL WITH** — A tip for pairing the dish with beer or wine or an additional food that would jazz up the meal a little.

Every recipe also includes one or more of the following labels, indicating its level of ease.

- **30 MINUTES OR LESS** — The recipe takes 30 minutes or less to make from start to finish.

- **5 INGREDIENTS OR FEWER** — The recipe requires 5 or fewer ingredients to assemble, excluding salt, black pepper, oil, and water.

- **ONE POT** — The recipe requires only one vessel to assemble, prepare, and cook.

Chapter 2

Lighter Fare

Tomato-Basil Bisque

SERVES 2 / PREP TIME: 5 MINUTES / COOK TIME: 15 MINUTES

This easy version of a delightful comfort food adds creaminess and protein with whole-milk Greek yogurt, an ingredient you can use up in other recipes. To make this dish vegan, swap out the yogurt for 8 ounces of silken tofu, and add it with the tomatoes in step 2. You can use an immersion blender for step 3 to save you from cleaning another vessel.

1 tablespoon avocado oil

½ yellow onion, diced

½ cup reduced-sodium vegetable broth

1 (14.5-ounce) can fire-roasted tomatoes

2 tablespoons tomato paste

1 teaspoon dried basil

½ teaspoon kosher salt

Pinch freshly ground black pepper

½ cup full-fat plain Greek yogurt

2 teaspoons balsamic vinegar

Per Serving: *Calories: 191; Fat: 11g; Carbohydrates: 17g; Fiber: 3g; Sugar: 10g; Protein: 8g; Sodium: 790mg*

1. In a Dutch oven or soup pot, heat the oil over medium heat until it shimmers. Add the onion, and sauté for 3 minutes, until soft.
2. Stir in the broth, roasted tomatoes, tomato paste, and basil. Season with the salt and pepper, and stir just until combined. Cover, and simmer for 10 minutes. Remove from the heat.
3. Carefully transfer to a blender, and add the yogurt. Place the lid on the blender but remove the plug. Hold a clean kitchen towel over the opening on the lid, leaving a small space for steam to escape. Blend for 30 to 60 seconds, until very smooth.
4. Divide the soup evenly between 2 bowls. Drizzle each with 1 teaspoon of vinegar.

PAIRS WELL WITH: Serve with crusty or toasted bread for dipping or a simple side salad.

Spicy Butternut Squash Soup

SERVES 2 / PREP TIME: 10 MINUTES / COOK TIME: 20 MINUTES

Butternut squash is delicious, but cutting it up can be annoying and time-consuming. Thanks to frozen squash, this creamy soup with a kick is now a speedy vegan dinner. Don't skip the splash of white-wine vinegar on top. It's the perfect touch of brightness to make this soup feel extra fancy.

1 tablespoon avocado oil

½ cup chopped yellow onion

2 garlic cloves, minced

1½ cups frozen butternut squash cubes

1¼ cups reduced-sodium vegetable broth

1 (15.5-ounce) can cannellini beans, rinsed and drained

¼ teaspoon kosher salt

⅛ teaspoon freshly ground black pepper

¼ teaspoon red pepper flakes

2 teaspoons white-wine vinegar

Per Serving: *Calories: 403; Fat: 8g; Carbohydrates: 67g; Fiber: 13g; Sugar: 6g; Protein: 19g; Sodium: 1,491mg*

1. In a Dutch oven or soup pot, heat the oil over medium heat until it shimmers.
2. Add the onion, and sauté for 3 minutes, until soft. Add the garlic, and sauté, stirring frequently, for another 1 minute, until fragrant.
3. Add the butternut squash, and cook for 3 minutes, until no longer frozen.
4. Add the broth, then stir in the beans. Season with the salt and pepper, and stir to combine. Cover, and bring to a boil. Reduce the heat to medium-low, and simmer for 5 minutes.
5. Stir in the red pepper flakes, and cook for another 3 minutes. Remove from the heat.
6. Carefully transfer to a blender. Place the lid on the blender but remove the plug. Hold a clean kitchen towel over the opening on the lid, leaving a small space for steam to escape. Blend for 1 to 2 minutes, until creamy.
7. Divide the soup evenly between 2 bowls. Drizzle each with 1 teaspoon of vinegar.

SWAP OR SUBSTITUTE: You can substitute the same amount of any winter squash, such as acorn or pumpkin, for the butternut squash.

Cauliflower Curry Soup

SERVES 2 / PREP TIME: 10 MINUTES / COOK TIME: 15 MINUTES

Cauliflower gets a boost from curry and other aromatics to become a flavorful, filling vegan soup. And there's no skimping on plant-based protein thanks to creamy cannellini beans. For an extra pop of earthy flavor and health benefits, add some turmeric right before serving.

1 tablespoon avocado oil

½ cup chopped onion

1 medium sweet apple, peeled and diced

2 cups chopped fresh or frozen cauliflower

1 garlic clove, minced

2 teaspoons curry powder

1¼ cups reduced-sodium vegetable broth

1 (15.5-ounce) can cannellini beans, rinsed and drained

½ teaspoon kosher salt

1 teaspoon ground turmeric (optional)

1. In a Dutch oven or soup pot, heat the oil over medium heat until it shimmers.
2. Add the onion, apple, cauliflower, and garlic, and sauté for 4 minutes, until soft.
3. Add the curry powder, and cook, stirring continuously, for 30 to 60 seconds, until fragrant.
4. Add the broth, then stir in the beans. Bring to a boil, reduce the heat to medium-low, and simmer for about 6 minutes. Add salt.
5. Stir in the turmeric (if using). Remove from the heat. Divide the soup evenly between 2 bowls.

PAIRS WELL WITH: For a perfect flavor pairing, enjoy a fruity chardonnay or lager beer with this savory soup.

Per Serving: *Calories: 449; Fat: 9g; Carbohydrates: 77g; Fiber: 18g; Sugar: 17g; Protein: 20g; Sodium: 1,741mg*

Chicken Salsa Verde Soup

SERVES 2 / PREP TIME: 5 MINUTES / COOK TIME: 20 MINUTES

Salsa verde is an all-green salsa that adds a lot of flavor to soup. Look for a brand that contains only vegetables, herbs, and seasoning. This is a great recipe to double for a larger crowd or make for leftover meals.

1 tablespoon avocado oil

1 (8- to 10-ounce) boneless, skinless chicken breast

Kosher salt

Freshly ground black pepper

1 (14.5-ounce) can fire-roasted tomatoes, juices drained by half

1 cup store-bought salsa verde

1 (14.5-ounce) can black beans, rinsed and drained

Per Serving: *Calories: 466; Fat: 11g; Carbohydrates: 49g; Fiber: 19g; Sugar: 8g; Protein: 39g; Sodium: 1,292mg*

1. In a small Dutch oven or stockpot, heat the oil over medium-high heat until it shimmers.
2. Season the chicken on both sides with salt and pepper. Add to the pot, and sear for 4 to 5 minutes on each side, until no longer pink inside. Transfer to a cutting board.
3. Reduce the heat to medium. In the same pot, combine the tomatoes with juice, salsa verde, and beans. Stir to combine. Cook, stirring occasionally, for 5 minutes.
4. Meanwhile, coarsely chop or shred the chicken. Add the shredded chicken to the pot, reduce the heat to medium-low, and simmer for about 5 minutes, until heated through. Remove from the heat. Divide the soup evenly between 2 bowls.

SWAP OR SUBSTITUTE: You can make this soup vegetarian by omitting the chicken and using vegetable broth. Bump up the fiber and plant-based protein by adding a can of another type of bean (such as pinto or kidney).

Noodle Soup

SERVES 2 / PREP TIME: 15 MINUTES / COOK TIME: 15 MINUTES

This soup is the perfect comfort meal on a cold day or when you're feeling under the weather. Mushrooms are an unsung hero in adding flavor to quick meals, and this recipe is an easy way to enjoy them. Make the dish vegan with vegetable broth, or increase the protein by adding chicken and using chicken broth.

6 ounces extra-firm tofu

3 scallions

2 teaspoons cornstarch

1 tablespoon avocado oil

2 carrots, diced
(about 1 cup)

1 cup sliced baby
portabella or white
mushrooms

3 cups reduced-sodium
vegetable or
chicken broth

3 ounces dried egg or
rice noodles

¼ teaspoon kosher salt
(optional)

1. Line a plate with a paper towel. Place the tofu on top, cover with another paper towel, and set a heavy plate on top. Drain for 10 minutes.

2. Meanwhile, trim and thinly slice the scallions, keeping the green and white parts separate.

3. Using a sharp knife, cut the tofu into ½-inch dice. Transfer to a shallow bowl or plate, and toss with the cornstarch.

4. In a Dutch oven or soup pot, heat the oil over medium heat until it shimmers. Add the tofu, and sear 2 minutes, turning occasionally. Transfer to a plate.

5. To the same pot, add the scallion whites, carrots, and mushrooms. Reduce the heat to medium-low, and cook, stirring frequently, for 3 minutes, until the vegetables have softened slightly.

Per Serving: *Calories: 352; Fat: 18g; Carbohydrates: 48g; Fiber: 4g; Sugar: 6g; Protein: 15g; Sodium: 758mg*

6. Add the broth, increase the heat to medium-high, and bring to a boil. Add the noodles, and cook according to the package instructions. Taste, and add the salt if desired. Remove from the heat.

7. Divide the tofu evenly between 2 bowls. Ladle the soup over the tofu, and garnish with the scallion greens.

MAKE IT EASIER: Instead of chopping up fresh vegetables, use a bag of frozen carrots, mushrooms, and more to make this recipe even quicker.

Warm Quinoa Salad

SERVES 2 / PREP TIME: 5 MINUTES / COOK TIME: 25 MINUTES

Quinoa is easy to cook and a good source of both protein and fiber. If you're not familiar with it, this recipe is a great place to start. The salad is an all-in-one balanced meal that makes great leftovers if you want to double the recipe. It's a vegan dish with plant-based protein from the edamame, but you could add chopped cooked chicken, too.

1 cup reduced-sodium vegetable broth

½ cup quinoa, rinsed and drained

1 cup frozen edamame

¼ cup water

3 cups packed spinach leaves, chopped into ribbons

¼ cup fresh sweet basil (about 12 large leaves), chopped into ribbons

1 teaspoon extra-virgin olive oil

1 tablespoon plus 1 teaspoon red-wine vinegar

½ cup dried cherries (preferably unsweetened)

½ teaspoon freshly ground black pepper

Per Serving: *Calories: 372; Fat: 8g; Carbohydrates: 62g; Fiber: 8g; Sugar: 25g; Protein: 14g; Sodium: 217mg*

1. In a medium pot, combine the broth and quinoa. Bring to a boil over medium-high heat. Reduce the heat to medium-low, and simmer, covered, for 15 to 20 minutes, or until the quinoa is tender and has absorbed most of the liquid.
2. Meanwhile, put the edamame in a medium bowl with the water. Microwave on High for 3 minutes. Drain.
3. When the quinoa is ready, turn off the heat. Fold in the spinach. Cover, and set aside for 3 minutes, until the spinach is wilted.
4. Fold in the edamame, basil, oil, vinegar, and cherries, and stir until combined. Season with the pepper, and stir well. Divide the salad evenly between 2 plates.

MAKE IT EASIER: Cut out all the cooking time by using 2 cups ready-to-eat cooked quinoa or a rice blend, found in the rice aisle at the grocery store.

Tempeh Salad with Yogurt Basil Dressing

SERVES 2 / PREP TIME: 15 MINUTES / COOK TIME: 5 MINUTES

Tempeh is an excellent plant-based protein option that is very quick to prepare. It also has a meaty texture and can be flavored with practically anything. In this recipe, a quick yogurt dressing enhances all the flavors.

Nonstick cooking spray, for coating the skillet

8 ounces tempeh, cut into ½-inch strips

½ teaspoon avocado oil

Kosher salt

Freshly ground black pepper

½ cup full-fat plain Greek yogurt

1 garlic clove, minced

2 tablespoons water, plus more as needed

1 tablespoon freshly squeezed lemon juice

1 teaspoon dried basil

3 cups packed mixed salad greens

½ cup sliced grape tomatoes

¼ cup finely diced red onion

½ cup unseasoned croutons (optional)

Per Serving: *Calories: 342; Fat: 13g; Carbohydrates: 29g; Fiber: 12g; Sugar: 6g; Protein: 30g; Sodium: 456mg*

1. Heat a small dry skillet over medium heat. Spray with cooking spray.

2. Brush the tempeh strips with the oil, and season with salt and pepper. Add to the skillet, and cook for 2 minutes on each side, until heated through. Remove from the heat, and set aside.

3. To make the dressing, in a small bowl, whisk together the yogurt, garlic, water, lemon juice, 2 pinches of pepper, and the basil. If you want a thinner consistency, add more water.

4. Assemble the salad: Divide the salad greens evenly between 2 plates. Top each with ¼ cup of tomatoes, 2 tablespoons of onion, and ¼ cup of croutons (if using). Split the tempeh evenly between the 2 plates. Drizzle with the yogurt dressing.

SWAP OR SUBSTITUTE: Tempeh is a great long-lasting protein to keep in your refrigerator and can be used in other recipes in this book, like Open-Face Tempeh Melts (page 43), but you can substitute any protein you like.

Poblano, Corn, and Shrimp Salad

SERVES 2 / PREP TIME: 10 MINUTES / COOK TIME: 10 MINUTES

This superfast salad is simple but so flavorful. Poblano peppers have mild heat that is not overpowering and really pulls everything together. If you can't find arugula, go for another hearty green like baby kale or chard, or use peppery watercress.

Nonstick cooking spray, for coating the skillet

8 ounces medium or large shrimp, peeled and deveined

Kosher salt

Freshly ground black pepper

1 teaspoon avocado oil

1 poblano pepper, seeded and diced

⅓ cup diced red onion

1 cup corn niblets, drained

3 cups packed coarsely chopped arugula

2 teaspoons extra-virgin olive oil

Per Serving: *Calories: 328; Fat: 9g; Carbohydrates: 38g; Fiber: 7g; Sugar: 16g; Protein: 29g; Sodium: 613mg*

1. Heat a medium dry skillet over medium heat. Spray with cooking spray.
2. Season the shrimp with salt and pepper. Add to the skillet, and cook for 1 minute on each side, just until the flesh is no longer pink. Using tongs, transfer to a plate.
3. In the same skillet, heat the oil over medium heat until it shimmers. Add the poblano and onion. Season with a pinch each of salt and pepper. Cook, stirring occasionally, for 6 minutes, until the vegetables have softened.
4. Stir in the corn, and cook for 1 to 2 minutes, just until warmed through. Turn off the heat, and return the shrimp to the skillet. Toss to combine.
5. Assemble the salad: Divide the arugula evenly between 2 plates. Top with the shrimp mixture. Drizzle each serving with 1 teaspoon of extra-virgin olive oil.

MAKE IT EASIER: Purchase frozen cooked shrimp, or ask the seafood department if they can steam the shrimp for you. Many grocery stores offer this service.

Avocado-Kale Salad with Seared Salmon

SERVES 2 / PREP TIME: 10 MINUTES / COOK TIME: 5 MINUTES

Raw kale can be tough to eat, literally. Massaging kale with avocado helps tenderize the leaves and makes them much more enjoyable. Searing is a super quick and flavorful method for preparing salmon, making this meal both hearty and fast.

2 (4-ounce) skin-on salmon fillets

Kosher salt

Freshly ground black pepper

1 tablespoon avocado oil

4 cups packed chopped kale leaves, stemmed

½ Hass avocado, pitted, peeled, and sliced

¼ cup chopped walnuts

2 tablespoons balsamic vinegar

Per Serving: *Calories: 393; Fat: 27g; Carbohydrates: 11g; Fiber: 5g; Sugar: 4g; Protein: 30g; Sodium: 398mg*

1. Heat a dry skillet over medium-high heat.
2. Using paper towels, pat dry the salmon fillets. Season the flesh side with salt and pepper.
3. Put the oil in the pan, and heat until it shimmers. Place the fillets, flesh-side down, and sear for 3 minutes, untouched, until they release easily from the skillet. Using a spatula, carefully flip, and cook for another 1 to 2 minutes, just until the fish flakes easily with a fork. Remove from the heat.
4. Meanwhile, in a medium bowl, combine the kale and avocado. Using your hands, gently massage the avocado into the kale for several minutes, until the kale is completely coated and feels more tender.
5. Divide the avocado-kale mixture evenly between 2 plates. Sprinkle each with 2 tablespoons of chopped walnuts. Top each with a salmon fillet. Drizzle each with 1 tablespoon of vinegar.

MAKE IT EASIER: Look for bags of pre-chopped kale in the salad section to make this meal come together even quicker.

Strawberry, Steak, and Farro Salad

SERVES 2 / PREP TIME: 5 MINUTES / COOK TIME: 25 MINUTES

Don't think you have time for a nice steak during the week? Think again. Top sirloin is an affordable, tender cut available at many grocery stores. It cooks in a snap on the stovetop and pairs beautifully with whole-grain farro and strawberries. One of my favorite combinations is strawberries and steak, and I hope you love it, too.

⅓ cup farro, rinsed and drained

1 cup vegetable stock

Kosher salt

1 tablespoon avocado oil

1 (6- to 7-ounce) beef top sirloin steak

Freshly ground black pepper

3 tablespoons red-wine vinegar

1 shallot, minced

½ cup dry red wine

2 cups or 16 small strawberries, hulled and sliced

3 cups packed spring salad mix

1. In a small stockpot, combine the farro, vegetable stock, and a pinch of salt over medium-high heat. Bring to a boil, then reduce the heat to medium-low. Cover, and simmer for 25 minutes, until the farro is tender and has absorbed most of the liquid. Remove from the heat.

2. Meanwhile, in a cast-iron skillet, heat the oil over high heat until it shimmers.

3. Season the steak with salt and pepper. Add to the skillet, and sear for 3 minutes on each side, until the internal temperature reaches 145°F (for medium doneness). Transfer to a cutting board, and let rest.

4. Reduce the skillet heat to medium-low. To make the sauce, add the vinegar and shallot. Cook, stirring up the browned bits at the bottom of the skillet using a wooden spoon, for 2 minutes, until the shallot is soft.

5. Stir in the wine and half of the strawberries. Cook for about 5 minutes, until the liquid is reduced by half and the strawberries are soft. Remove from the heat.

Per Serving: *Calories: 396;*
Fat: 12g; Carbohydrates:
41g; Fiber: 9g; Sugar: 11g;
Protein: 23g; Sodium: 418mg

6. Assemble the salad: Using a serrated knife and cutting against the grain, cut the steak into thin strips. Divide the salad mix evenly between 2 plates. Using a slotted spoon, top the greens with the farro and remaining strawberries. Arrange the sliced steak on top, then ladle on the strawberry sauce.

SWAP OR SUBSTITUTE: If you don't have farro, substitute an equal amount of quinoa, barley, or brown rice.

Chapter 3

Vegetarian and Vegan

Broccoli-Cherry Quinoa Bowls

SERVES 2 / PREP TIME: 10 MINUTES / COOK TIME: 20 MINUTES

Quinoa contains a good amount of protein on its own, but adding chickpeas kicks it up a notch (and warming up the chickpeas while cooking the quinoa saves both time and another dish). The dried cherries balance out the broccoli nicely with a touch of sweetness.

FOR THE VEGGIE BOWL

½ cup quinoa, rinsed and drained

1 cup reduced-sodium vegetable broth

1 (15.5-ounce) can chickpeas, rinsed and drained

2 cups chopped broccoli

1 tablespoon extra-virgin olive oil

¼ teaspoon kosher salt

¼ teaspoon freshly ground black pepper

¼ cup pecans, chopped

2 tablespoons dried cherries (preferably unsweetened), chopped

1. **MAKE THE VEGGIE BOWL:** Preheat the oven to 450°F. Line a baking sheet with parchment paper.

2. In a small pot, combine the quinoa and broth, and bring to a boil over medium-high heat. Reduce the heat to medium-low, cover, and simmer for 10 minutes. Stir in the chickpeas, cover, and cook for another 5 minutes, until the quinoa is tender and has absorbed most of the liquid. Remove from the heat.

3. Meanwhile, put the broccoli on the prepared baking sheet. Sprinkle with the oil, salt, and pepper. Using tongs, toss until well coated. Spread out the broccoli in a single layer. Roast for 8 minutes, until tips are slightly charred. Remove from the oven.

FOR THE VINAIGRETTE

2 tablespoons
extra-virgin olive oil

2 teaspoons
Dijon mustard

2 teaspoons apricot
preserves

Per Serving: *Calories: 670; Fat: 37g; Carbohydrates: 72g; Fiber: 15g; Sugar: 12g; Protein: 19g; Sodium: 1,000mg*

4. **MEANWHILE, MAKE THE VINAIGRETTE:** In a small bowl, whisk together the extra-virgin olive oil, mustard, and apricot preserves.

5. Divide the quinoa-chickpea mixture evenly between 2 bowls. Top with the broccoli, pecans, and cherries. Drizzle with the vinaigrette.

MAKE IT EASIER: Purchase microwavable grain pouches to cut down on the cook time. Simply toss the chickpeas with the hot grain to warm them up.

USE IT UP: Apricot preserves are also used in Tuna Cakes with Apricot Dipping Sauce (page 72) and Apricot Chicken with Spinach Rice (page 84).

Chickpea Bites with Yogurt-Cucumber Sauce

SERVES 2 / PREP TIME: 15 MINUTES / COOK TIME: 10 MINUTES

If you're craving something along the lines of falafel, you'll love this recipe. For the best texture, use a food processor, but you can mash everything by hand, too. If you'd like a heartier meal, swap out the cauliflower rice for regular rice. Eat this all together in a bowl, or dip the chickpea bites in the yogurt sauce.

FOR THE CHICKPEA BITES

1 (15.5-ounce) can chickpeas, rinsed and drained

Juice of ½ lemon

1 garlic clove, minced

½ teaspoon dried oregano

1 teaspoon olive oil

1 large egg, beaten

⅓ cup old-fashioned oats

2 portions or 1 (10-ounce) bag frozen cauliflower rice

1. **MAKE THE CHICKPEA BITES:** Preheat the oven to 425°F. Line a baking sheet with parchment paper.

2. Put the chickpeas in a large bowl. Using a potato masher, mash them until lumpy. Add the lemon juice, garlic, oregano, oil, egg, and oats, and stir until well combined. Using your hands, form 8 equal-size balls, about 2 tablespoons each.

3. Place the chickpea balls on the prepared baking sheet, spacing about 2 inches apart. Bake for 10 minutes, until browned and crispy. Remove from the oven.

FOR THE YOGURT-CUCUMBER SAUCE

½ cup full-fat
Greek yogurt

Juice of ½ lemon

½ cup shredded
field cucumber

½ teaspoon dried dill

Pinch kosher salt

Per Serving: Calories: 394; Fat: 12g; Carbohydrates: 52g; Fiber: 13g; Sugar: 12g; Protein: 24g; Sodium: 439mg

4. **MAKE THE YOGURT-CUCUMBER SAUCE:** In a bowl, mix together the yogurt, lemon juice, cucumber, dill, and salt.

5. Heat the cauliflower rice according to the package instructions.

6. Divide the cauliflower rice evenly between 2 bowls. Top each with 4 chickpea bites and a dollop of yogurt-cucumber sauce.

MAKE IT EASIER: If you're short on time or patience, simply toss together whole chickpeas, lemon juice, garlic, oregano, and olive oil (omit the egg and oats), and heat in the microwave. Spoon over cauliflower for a really fast bowl.

Quick Chickpea Curry

SERVES 2 / PREP TIME: 10 MINUTES / COOK TIME: 15 MINUTES

If you have a hankering for curry, are short on time, or have an overflowing produce bin in your refrigerator, this recipe is for you. You can use almost any vegetable, whether fresh, canned, or frozen. Curry paste is widely available at grocery stores. Pick the type you prefer: red curry tends to be spicier, and yellow curry is generally milder. This recipe is naturally vegan and gluten-free, but check the ingredients on the curry paste to be sure.

1 tablespoon avocado oil

1 to 2 tablespoons curry paste (red, green, or yellow, as desired)

½ small yellow onion, sliced

1 garlic clove, chopped

2 cups assorted chopped vegetables, like broccoli, cauliflower, carrots, or celery

1 (15.5-ounce) can chickpeas, rinsed and drained

⅔ cup canned light coconut milk

1 teaspoon ground turmeric

⅓ cup fresh basil leaves, chopped (optional)

Per Serving: *Calories: 369; Fat: 17g; Carbohydrates: 42g; Fiber: 14g; Sugar: 4g; Protein: 15g; Sodium: 829mg*

1. In a medium skillet, heat the oil over medium heat until it shimmers.

2. Stir in the curry paste, and toast for 30 seconds, until fragrant. Add the onion, garlic, and vegetables, and stir until well coated. Cook, stirring occasionally, for about 8 minutes, until crisp-tender.

3. Add the chickpeas, coconut milk, and turmeric, and stir to combine. Reduce the heat to medium-low, and simmer, uncovered, for about 5 minutes, until heated through. Remove from the heat. Divide the curry evenly between 2 plates. Garnish with the basil (if using).

PAIRS WELL WITH: Add any additional protein you like to this dish—chicken, steak, or shrimp all work well. You can also serve it over a grain like quinoa, rice, or noodles for a heartier meal.

Pick-Your-Flavor Bean Burger

SERVES 2 / PREP TIME: 10 MINUTES / COOK TIME: 10 MINUTES

This bean burger is sure to become your go-to. It's stuffed with vegetables, and you can season it so many different ways. Make these burgers totally vegan by using an egg substitute and choosing a vegan cheese slice or omitting the cheese entirely.

1 (14.5-ounce) can black beans, rinsed and drained

¼ cup plain dry bread crumbs

½ cup grated yellow onion

½ cup grated carrot (or cut into matchsticks)

1 teaspoon garlic powder

⅛ teaspoon kosher salt

Seasoning of choice: 1 to 2 teaspoons grated lime zest, 2 teaspoons sriracha, 1 teaspoon smoked paprika, or 1 tablespoon barbecue sauce (optional)

1 large egg

1 tablespoon avocado oil

2 thin slices cheese of your choice (optional)

4 butter or green-leaf lettuce leaves

Per Serving: *Calories: 502; Fat: 20g; Carbohydrates: 55g; Fiber: 18g; Sugar: 5g; Protein: 26g; Sodium: 724mg*

1. Put the beans in a medium bowl. Using a potato masher, mash them until lumpy (it's okay if not all beans are fully mashed).
2. Add the bread crumbs, onion, carrot, garlic powder, salt, seasoning of choice (if using), and egg. Stir until well combined. Using your hands, divide the mixture into 4 equal portions, and form flattened patties.
3. In a medium skillet, heat the oil over medium heat until it shimmers. Add the patties, and cook for 3 to 4 minutes on each side, until browned and cooked through. Top each with ½ slice of cheese during the final minute of cooking (if using).
4. Remove from the heat, and let rest until slightly cooled. Place each patty in a lettuce leaf.

USE IT UP: Use the leftover carrots from this recipe in Mediterranean-Style Chicken Bowls (page 88). Prep a quick salad with the leftover lettuce, or use it in Beef Lettuce Wraps (page 122).

Bean Empanadas

SERVES 2 / PREP TIME: 10 MINUTES / COOK TIME: 20 MINUTES

Empanadas are a favorite in my house. In this version, I swapped out ground beef for creamy pinto beans. You'll find frozen empanada discs in the international section of frozen foods. Defrost them in the refrigerator, and keep them there until you're ready to add the filling. Empanadas are typically fried, but I've figured out how to bake them and still get the iconic crunch.

1 tablespoon avocado oil

1 small green bell pepper, seeded and diced (about ¾ cup)

¼ cup diced onion

1 (14.5-ounce) can pinto beans, rinsed and drained

2 garlic cloves, minced

⅓ cup raisins

½ teaspoon ground cumin

2 tablespoons tomato paste

⅓ cup beer (like a pale ale) or no-sodium-added vegetable broth

¼ teaspoon kosher salt

¼ teaspoon freshly ground black pepper

6 (5-inch) frozen empanada discs, thawed

Per Serving: *Calories: 668; Fat: 19g; Carbohydrates: 113g; Fiber: 14g; Sugar: 21g; Protein: 22g; Sodium: 713mg*

1. In a medium skillet, heat the oil over medium heat until it shimmers. Add the bell pepper and onion, and sauté for 2 minutes, until the vegetables have softened.

2. Stir in the beans, garlic, raisins, cumin, tomato paste, beer, salt, and black pepper. Bring to a simmer, and cook for 3 to 4 minutes, until the beer has been reduced by half. Remove from the heat.

3. Meanwhile, preheat the oven to 450°F. Line a baking sheet with parchment paper.

4. Top each empanada disc with ¼ cup of the filling. Fold the empanadas in half, and using a fork, press the edges together to seal.

5. Arrange the stuffed empanadas in a single layer on the prepared baking sheet. Bake for 12 to 14 minutes, or until golden brown. Remove from the oven.

PAIRS WELL WITH: Serve with salsa, guacamole, chips, and your favorite beer.

Black Bean–Stuffed Bell Peppers with Plantains

Black beans with plantains is one of my favorite vegetarian dinners. Baking the plantains, instead of frying, makes them easier to enjoy at home. Look for yellow plantains with lots of brown spots, or buy them early in the week and let them ripen on the counter.

1 (14.5-ounce) can black beans, rinsed and drained

½ cup store-bought salsa verde

2 large green or red bell peppers, halved lengthwise and seeded

1 large very ripe plantain

1 teaspoon avocado oil

Per Serving: *Calories: 412; Fat: 4g; Carbohydrates: 83g; Fiber: 21g; Sugar: 25g; Protein: 16g; Sodium: 496mg*

1. Preheat the oven to 375°F. Line a baking sheet with parchment paper.
2. In a medium bowl, mix together the beans and salsa verde. Stuff each bell pepper half with one-quarter of the bean mixture. Place the stuffed bell peppers on one side of the pre-pared baking sheet.
3. Slice through the plantain peel lengthwise, from top to bottom, then remove. Using a sharp knife, slice the plantain on an angle to make ¼-inch-thick rounds. Arrange the slices in a single layer on the other side of the baking sheet. Drizzle with the oil.
4. Bake for 15 minutes, flip the plantains, and bake for another 10 to 15 minutes, until the bell peppers are cooked through and the plantains are golden. Remove from the oven.
5. Divide the stuffed bell peppers evenly between 2 plates, and serve with a side of plantains.

PAIRS WELL WITH: If you like rice with your beans, add ½ cup rice per person to this meal. You can also serve it with a handful of tortilla chips.

USE IT UP: Use extra salsa verde in Chicken Salsa Verde Soup (page 21).

Chipotle Lentil Tacos

SERVES 2 / PREP TIME: 5 MINUTES / COOK TIME: 30 MINUTES

This recipe might become your go-to vegetarian taco. Lentils are a nutritional powerhouse full of protein, fiber, and other important nutrients. You can use these lentils on top of rice, salad, or chips, or eat them all by themselves. I like to make a batch of these tacos on the weekend for easy weekday lunches. Use corn tortillas to make this dish gluten-free.

2 cups reduced-sodium vegetable broth

1 cup dried brown or green lentils

½ teaspoon chipotle pepper powder

1 teaspoon garlic powder

½ teaspoon smoked paprika

½ teaspoon kosher salt

4 (8- or 10-inch) whole-wheat or corn tortillas

¼ cup full-fat sour cream

1 cup shredded Mexican-style cheese blend

1 cup diced seeded tomatoes

1. In a medium pot, combine the broth, lentils, chipotle powder, garlic powder, smoked paprika, and salt. Bring to a boil over medium-high heat.
2. Reduce the heat to medium-low, cover, and simmer for 30 minutes, until the lentils are tender and have absorbed most of the liquid. Remove from the heat.
3. Fill each tortilla with one-quarter of the lentils (about ½ cup), 1 tablespoon of sour cream, ¼ cup of shredded cheese, and ¼ cup of tomatoes. Add more toppings if desired.

USE IT UP: Use up extra lentils in Spiced Lentils with Acorn Squash (page 41) and the chipotle pepper powder in Cornmeal-Crusted Flounder with Zucchini (page 73).

Per Serving: *Calories: 881; Fat: 29g; Carbohydrates: 110g; Fiber: 20g; Sugar: 9g; Protein: 48g; Sodium: 1,482mg*

Spiced Lentils with Acorn Squash

The flavors in this lentil dish are a nod to the comfort of the cooler seasons, but you can enjoy this recipe any time of year. I think it feels like a warm hug for your belly. This meal is vegan and gluten-free.

1 small acorn squash, halved and seeded

1¾ cups reduced-sodium vegetable broth, divided

1 tablespoon pure maple syrup

¾ cup dried brown or green lentils

¼ teaspoon ground nutmeg

Pinch ground cardamom (optional)

Per Serving: *Calories: 362; Fat: 1g; Carbohydrates: 79g; Fiber: 11g; Sugar: 9g; Protein: 20g; Sodium: 494mg*

1. Preheat the oven to 425°F.
2. Using a sharp knife, cut the acorn squash into 8 wedges.
3. Pour ¼ cup of broth into a 2-quart casserole dish or an 8-by-8-inch pan. Place the acorn squash, skin-side down, in the dish. Drizzle with the maple syrup.
4. Bake for about 25 minutes, until the squash is tender and easily pierced with a fork. Remove from the oven.
5. Meanwhile, in a small pot, combine the lentils and remaining 1½ cups of broth, and bring to a boil over medium-high heat. Reduce the heat to medium-low, cover, and simmer for 15 minutes (check periodically, and add more broth if the lentils become dry). The lentils are cooked when they are tender and have absorbed most of the liquid. Add the nutmeg and cardamom (if using), and stir until well combined. Remove from the heat.
6. Divide the acorn squash evenly between 2 plates, and spoon the lentils over the top.

MAKE IT EASIER: You can also use precut winter squash of any type, including butternut or delicata squash, and roast it on a baking sheet.

Sweet Potato Hash

SERVES 2 / PREP TIME: 10 MINUTES / COOK TIME: 20 MINUTES

This dish is not your everyday sweet potato hash. A unique mix of vegetables and a touch of sweetness from hoisin sauce make it extra special. As an added bonus, the recipe is naturally vegan.

2 medium sweet potatoes, peeled and diced (about 2 cups)

1 teaspoon extra-virgin olive oil

⅛ teaspoon kosher salt

⅛ teaspoon freshly ground black pepper

½ cup frozen edamame

2 small or medium red bell peppers, seeded and chopped

1 cup quartered mushrooms

2 tablespoons hoisin sauce

1 tablespoon toasted sesame seeds (optional)

Per Serving: *Calories: 259; Fat: 7g; Carbohydrates: 43g; Fiber: 8g; Sugar: 15g; Protein: 9g; Sodium: 484mg*

1. Preheat the oven to 450°F. Line a baking sheet with parchment paper.
2. In a large bowl, combine the sweet potatoes, oil, salt, and black pepper. Toss until well coated. Arrange in an even layer on half of the prepared baking sheet. Bake for 15 minutes.
3. Meanwhile, in a medium bowl, combine the edamame, bell peppers, mushrooms, and hoisin sauce. Toss well.
4. Remove the baking sheet from the oven. Spread the edamame mixture on the other side of the baking sheet. Return to the oven, and bake for another 5 minutes, until the vegetables have softened. Remove from the oven.
5. Divide the vegetables evenly between 2 bowls. Sprinkle with the sesame seeds (if using).

MAKE IT EASIER: Buy precut onions, peppers, mushrooms, and sweet potatoes to greatly reduce your prep time.

Open-Face Tempeh Melts

SERVES 2 / PREP TIME: 15 MINUTES / COOK TIME: 5 MINUTES

A warm sandwich for dinner can hit the spot after a long day. This vegetarian melt is loaded with vegetables, including superfood sprouts. Look for alfalfa or broccoli sprouts in the produce section of your grocery store. If you can, prepare the tempeh in the morning; a long marinade will help the flavor of the vinaigrette really sink in.

8 ounces tempeh

¼ cup store-bought Italian vinaigrette

2 thick whole-grain bread slices, cut in half

¼ cup store-bought hummus

1 medium tomato, sliced

1 cup alfalfa sprouts

2 provolone or sharp cheddar cheese slices, cut in half

Per Serving: *Calories: 569; Fat: 25g; Carbohydrates: 51g; Fiber: 16g; Sugar: 9g; Protein: 39g; Sodium: 750mg*

1. Crumble the tempeh into a medium bowl. Add the vinaigrette, and toss to coat.
2. Preheat the oven to 375°F. On a small baking sheet, arrange the bread slices in a single layer. Toast for 1 minute on each side.
3. Remove from the oven, and keep the oven on. Spread 1 tablespoon of hummus on each piece of toast. Top with the tomato slices. Spoon the tempeh out of the marinade, shaking off any excess, and spread over the tomato. Top each with the sprouts and half a cheese slice.
4. Return to the oven. Bake for another 3 minutes, until the cheese is melted and the tempeh is warm. Remove from the oven. Serve immediately.

USE IT UP: Have leftover tempeh and sprouts? Serve them over salad greens, or stuff them in a tortilla for a quick lunch the next day. If you have extra bread, use it for Shrimp Panzanella (page 58).

Teriyaki Tofu Stir-Fry

SERVES 2 / PREP TIME: 15 MINUTES / COOK TIME: 15 MINUTES

Tofu can taste great with the help of a good sauce and a little sear in a hot pan. I like P.F. Chang's teriyaki sauce, which can be found in well-stocked grocery stores. It's important to use extra-firm tofu in this recipe and press it before cooking so it stays together. You can use any combo of stir-fry vegetables you like, fresh or frozen. If you opt for fresh, about 2 cups is a good starting amount, but feel free to add more. This recipe is vegan.

1 (7- to 8-ounce) block extra-firm tofu

1 tablespoon cornstarch

2 tablespoons avocado oil, divided

1 (10-ounce) bag frozen stir-fry vegetables

¼ cup teriyaki sauce

1 (8.8-ounce) pouch microwavable brown rice

1. Line a plate with a paper towel. Place the tofu on top, cover with another paper towel, and set a heavy plate on top. Drain for 10 minutes.

2. Cut the tofu into ½-inch dice, and transfer to a shallow bowl or plate. Toss with the cornstarch.

3. In a small skillet, heat 1 tablespoon of oil over medium heat until it shimmers. Add the tofu, and cook for about 2 minutes per side on at least 2 sides, until browned (wait to flip until the tofu releases easily from the skillet). Transfer to a plate.

4. If the skillet is dry, add the remaining 1 tablespoon of oil. Add the vegetables, and cook for about 3 minutes, until they have warmed up and show brown marks. Add the teriyaki sauce, and stir to combine. Turn off the heat. Return the tofu to the skillet, and toss to coat in the sauce.

Per Serving: *Calories: 515; Fat: 20g; Carbohydrates: 63g; Fiber: 10g; Sugar: 10g; Protein: 19g; Sodium: 1,434mg*

5. Prepare the rice according to the package instructions.
6. Divide the rice evenly between 2 bowls. Top with the tofu stir-fry.

USE IT UP: If you have fresh or frozen vegetables you need to use up, this recipe tastes great with almost anything. You can also add any leftover rice or grain you have on hand.

Sweet Potato, Kale, and Egg Stacks

SERVES 2 / PREP TIME: 10 MINUTES / COOK TIME: 15 MINUTES

This satisfying meal is loaded with flavor, and charred kale is a game changer. Cook your eggs however you enjoy them, but a runny yoke is my favorite style.

1 large sweet potato (or 2 small), peeled and diced

¼ cup water

Nonstick cooking spray, for coating

½ small yellow or sweet onion, diced

1 tablespoon avocado oil, plus 1 teaspoon

¼ teaspoon kosher salt

¼ teaspoon freshly ground black pepper

3 cups packed chopped kale leaves

2 large eggs

½ cup shredded sharp cheddar cheese

1. Put the sweet potato in a microwave-safe bowl, and add the water. Microwave on High for 5 minutes, until mostly soft. Drain.

2. Position an oven rack about 7 inches from the broiler. Preheat the broiler to high. Line a rimmed baking sheet with aluminum foil, and spray with cooking spray.

3. Combine the sweet potato and onion on the prepared baking sheet. Drizzle with 1 tablespoon of oil, and season with the salt and pepper. Using tongs, toss until well coated. Spread out the vegetables in a single layer. Broil, watching carefully and stirring occasionally, for about 8 to 10 minutes, until the sweet potato is crispy and lightly charred. Remove from the oven.

4. Meanwhile, in a medium skillet, heat the remaining 1 teaspoon of oil over medium-high heat. Add the kale, and cook for about 5 minutes, until charred. Transfer to a plate.

Per Serving: *Calories: 406; Fat: 24g; Carbohydrates: 32g; Fiber: 5g; Sugar: 8g; Protein: 16g; Sodium: 627mg*

5. Reduce the heat to medium. Spray the skillet with cooking spray. Add the eggs, and fry to desired doneness. Remove from the heat.

6. Dividing evenly between 2 plates, layer the sweet potato and onion, charred kale, and cooked eggs, then top with the shredded cheese to make stacks.

SWAP OR SUBSTITUTE: Use any type of white potato you like. Check for doneness since cook time may vary. Feel free to add more than one egg to each stack.

Zucchini and Sun-Dried Tomato Mini Frittatas

SERVES 2 / PREP TIME: 10 MINUTES / COOK TIME: 20 MINUTES

Eggs are an excellent choice for a quick dinner. These mini frittatas have vegetables baked right in for an all-in-one meal. Round things out with a slice of toast if you like a little crunch.

Nonstick cooking spray, for coating the muffin tin

½ cup grated zucchini (about half a zucchini)

3 large eggs

¼ cup 2 percent milk

1 garlic clove, minced

Kosher salt

Freshly ground black pepper

2 tablespoons chopped sun-dried tomatoes

¼ cup shredded cheddar cheese

Per Serving: *Calories: 201; Fat: 13g; Carbohydrates: 5g; Fiber: 1g; Sugar: 3g; Protein: 15g; Sodium: 233mg*

1. Preheat the oven to 350°F. Coat 4 cups of a standard muffin tin with cooking spray.
2. Wrap the grated zucchini in a paper towel, and gently squeeze over the sink to remove excess moisture.
3. In a medium bowl, whisk together the eggs, milk, garlic, and salt and pepper to taste for 2 minutes, until the eggs are foamy.
4. Pour 1 tablespoon of the egg mixture into each prepared muffin cup. Divide the zucchini evenly among the cups, fanning out the shreds. Top with the sun-dried tomatoes.
5. Pour in the rest of the egg mixture, filling each muffin cup to the top. Sprinkle each with about 1 tablespoon of cheese.
6. Bake for 16 to 17 minutes, or until the frittatas are firm and slightly browned.
7. Remove from the oven, and let sit for 1 minute. Using a knife or small spatula, loosen the frittatas from the sides, and lift out of the muffin cups.

USE IT UP: The other zucchini half can be used in Teriyaki Shrimp and Veggie Bowls (page 62) or Shrimp Panzanella (page 58). Use extra sun-dried tomatoes in Spinach-Artichoke Pasta (page 50).

Banana-Oat Cakes

SERVES 2 / PREP TIME: 5 MINUTES / COOK TIME: 25 MINUTES

Breakfast for dinner is always a great idea. These oat cakes are a good source of fiber and provide satisfying protein. Top with your favorite fruit for a delicious and quick meal.

1 medium ripe banana, peeled

1 (5.3-ounce) carton full-fat vanilla Greek yogurt

1 large egg

1½ cups old-fashioned oats

½ teaspoon baking soda

1 teaspoon ground cinnamon

Pinch kosher salt

Nonstick cooking spray, for coating the skillet

1 cup sliced strawberries or bananas (optional)

Per Serving: *Calories: 397; Fat: 4g; Carbohydrates: 64g; Fiber: 10g; Sugar: 14g; Protein: 19g; Sodium: 455mg*

1. Heat a dry medium skillet over medium-low heat.
2. In a mixing bowl, mash the banana using a fork or potato masher. Stir in the yogurt and egg, then fold in the oats, baking soda, cinnamon, and salt.
3. Spray the hot skillet with cooking spray. Scoop about ⅓ cup of the batter onto the skillet, and gently flatten using the back of a spoon or spatula. Cook for about 2 minutes on each side, until golden brown. Transfer to a plate, and tent with aluminum foil to keep warm. Continue with the remaining batter. You should have about 6 pancakes total. Turn off the heat.
4. Serve with the strawberries or bananas (if using).

SWAP OR SUBSTITUTE: For a fun flavor twist, swap in flavored yogurt for the vanilla—banana is a favorite in my house. These pancakes are already low in added sugar, but if you want to decrease it even more, opt for plain Greek yogurt.

Spinach-Artichoke Pasta

SERVES 2 / PREP TIME: 5 MINUTES / COOK TIME: 15 MINUTES

Artichokes don't just taste great, they also contain fiber that can help your gut health. This pasta provides an easy, delicious way to enjoy them regularly, along with more greens from spinach.

¾ cup dried high-protein penne or casarecce pasta

1 teaspoon avocado oil

4 garlic cloves, finely chopped

¼ cup sun-dried tomatoes, julienned

1 (6- to 7-ounce) jar or can marinated artichoke hearts, drained

½ cup dry white wine, like chardonnay

¼ teaspoon freshly ground black pepper

3 cups packed spinach leaves

¼ cup freshly grated Parmesan cheese

Per Serving: *Calories: 280; Fat: 6g; Carbohydrates: 45g; Fiber: 8g; Sugar: 5g; Protein: 14g; Sodium: 271mg*

1. Bring a medium pot of water to a boil over high heat. Add the penne, and cook to al dente according to the package instructions. Remove from the heat. Drain, reserving ½ cup of the pasta cooking water.

2. In a medium skillet, heat the oil over medium heat until it shimmers. Add the garlic, and sauté for 1 minute, until fragrant.

3. Add the sun-dried tomatoes, artichoke hearts, wine, and pepper, and stir well. Cook for about 6 minutes, until the wine is reduced by half.

4. Turn off the heat. Add the penne and spinach, and stir until the spinach is wilted. If the pasta seems too dry, add the reserved pasta cooking water, 1 tablespoon at a time, until you achieve the desired consistency.

5. Divide the pasta evenly between 2 bowls. Sprinkle each with 2 tablespoons of cheese.

PAIRS WELL WITH: Try adding even more vegetables to this pasta, such as asparagus or mushrooms.

USE IT UP: Excess white wine can be used up in Parmesan Chicken over Wild Rice (page 92) or Mussels in White Wine–Tomato Broth with Potatoes (page 56).

Roasted Cauliflower Pasta

SERVES 2 / PREP TIME: 5 MINUTES / COOK TIME: 15 MINUTES

This pasta recipe is so simple but has so much flavor. Cauliflower is not the most beloved vegetable because it can be bitter, but this recipe totally redeems it. You can swap in an equal amount of fresh cauliflower for the frozen.

½ large red onion, cut into 1-inch pieces (about 1 cup)

1 (10-ounce) bag frozen cauliflower

1 tablespoon extra-virgin olive oil, plus 1 teaspoon

¼ teaspoon kosher salt

¼ teaspoon freshly ground black pepper

1 cup dried high-protein penne pasta

½ cup freshly grated Parmesan cheese

3 tablespoons plain dry bread crumbs

Per Serving: *Calories: 520; Fat: 20g; Carbohydrates: 62g; Fiber: 6g; Sugar: 8g; Protein: 24g; Sodium: 1,037mg*

1. Preheat the oven to 450°F. Line a baking sheet with aluminum foil.
2. Combine the onion, cauliflower, 1 tablespoon of oil, the salt, and pepper on the prepared baking sheet. Using tongs, toss until well coated. Spread out the vegetables in a single layer. Roast for 15 minutes, until tender and slightly browned. Remove from the oven.
3. Meanwhile, bring a medium pot of water to a boil over high heat. Add the penne, and cook to al dente according to the package instructions. Remove from the heat. Drain, reserving ½ cup of the pasta cooking water, and return the penne to the pot.
4. Add the roasted cauliflower mixture, cheese, remaining 1 teaspoon of oil, and the bread crumbs. Toss together. If the pasta seems too dry, add the reserved pasta cooking water, 1 tablespoon at a time, until you achieve the desired consistency.
5. Divide the pasta evenly between 2 bowls.

PAIRS WELL WITH: Any type of cooked protein can be added to this dish, like chicken, shrimp, or sausage.

Veggie Skillet Lasagna

SERVES 2 / PREP TIME: 10 MINUTES / COOK TIME: 20 MINUTES

My friend Kathy asked me to add a vegetable lasagna to this book. It's one of her favorite meals, but she's a recent empty nester and no longer needs to make a whole pan. This recipe is dedicated to her and anyone else who just wants veggie lasagna for one day, not 10. Feel free to add more vegetables than those listed here. (If any of them have a high water content, squeeze over the sink before adding to the sauce.)

1 teaspoon avocado oil

½ cup shredded and squeezed zucchini

½ cup shredded carrot

¼ cup diced onion

1 cup finely chopped kale

2 cups marinara sauce

3 (6½-inch-by-3½-inch) sheets no-cook lasagna noodles

¾ cup ricotta cheese

½ cup shredded mozzarella cheese

2 tablespoons freshly grated Parmesan cheese (optional)

Per Serving: *Calories: 592; Fat: 25g; Carbohydrates: 63g; Fiber: 10g; Sugar: 17g; Protein: 27g; Sodium: 443mg*

1. In a 2-quart oven-safe pot, heat the oil over medium heat. Add the zucchini, carrot, onion, and kale, and sauté for about 4 minutes, until tender. Stir in the marinara sauce.
2. Break the lasagna sheets into thirds, and gently submerge them in the sauce. Cover, reduce the heat to medium-low, and cook for 10 minutes, until the sheets are al dente.
3. Position an oven rack about 7 inches from the broiler. Preheat the broiler to high.
4. Turn off the stove, and remove the lid. Drop in the ricotta cheese by the spoonful, then gently swirl into the sauce. Sprinkle the top with the mozzarella cheese.
5. Broil for about 2 minutes, until the cheese is bubbly and slightly browned. Remove from the oven.
6. Let cool slightly. Divide the lasagna evenly between 2 bowls, and sprinkle with the Parmesan cheese (if using).

PAIRS WELL WITH: Serve with a Caesar salad or the salad kit of your choice.

Chapter 4
Fish and Seafood

Mussels in White Wine–Tomato Broth with Potatoes

SERVES 2 / PREP TIME: 5 MINUTES / COOK TIME: 25 MINUTES

If you love mussels, there's no need to wait for a trip to an expensive restaurant. They steam on the stovetop in minutes and make for a perfect main meal for two. They are also a great source of iron, magnesium, zinc, vitamin B_1, and vitamin B_{12}.

1 medium red potato, cut into ½-inch-thick sticks

2 teaspoons avocado oil, divided

1 teaspoon garlic powder

1 teaspoon kosher salt, divided

½ teaspoon freshly ground black pepper, divided

1 pound mussels, debearded

5 garlic cloves, chopped

1 medium zucchini, diced

¾ cup dry white wine, like chardonnay

1 (14.5-ounce) can diced tomatoes with their juices

1. Preheat the oven to 450°F. Line a baking sheet with parchment paper.

2. Put the potato sticks on the prepared baking sheet. Drizzle with 1 teaspoon of oil, and season with the garlic powder, ½ teaspoon of salt, and ¼ teaspoon of pepper. Using tongs, toss until well coated. Spread out the potato sticks in a single layer. Bake for 23 to 25 minutes, flipping halfway through, until tender on the inside and browned on the outside. Remove from the oven.

3. Meanwhile, soak the mussels in a bowl of water for 5 minutes.

4. In a Dutch oven or large pot with a lid, heat the remaining 1 teaspoon of oil over medium heat until it shimmers. Add the garlic and zucchini, and cook for 1 minute, until fragrant.

5. Add the wine, tomatoes with their juices, and the remaining ½ teaspoon of salt and ¼ teaspoon of pepper. Stir to combine.

6. Increase the heat to high, and bring the mixture to a boil. Reduce the heat to medium-low, and simmer for 3 minutes to let the flavors meld.

Per Serving: *Calories: 470; Fat: 13g; Carbohydrates: 55g; Fiber: 8g; Sugar: 8g; Protein: 34g; Sodium: 1,292mg*

7. Drain the mussels, and add to the pot. Cover, and steam for 3 minutes, until the mussels have fully opened. Discard any mussels that do not open after about 5 minutes. Remove from the heat.

8. Divide the mussels, broth, and vegetables evenly between 2 bowls, with the potatoes on the side.

SWAP OR SUBSTITUTE: You can add even more vegetables to the broth as desired, or swap out the zucchini for yellow squash, diced carrots, diced celery, or a frozen vegetable mix.

Shrimp Panzanella

SERVES 2 / PREP TIME: 10 MINUTES / COOK TIME: 15 MINUTES

Panzanella is a salad made with bread. This recipe includes a quick method for turning leftover bread into crunchy croutons. It's a great way to use up the last bit of a loaf and make an all-in-one meal. You can easily add more vegetables, like sliced carrots or broccoli, to this dish.

2 thick whole-grain bread slices, cut into ½-inch cubes

1 tablespoon avocado oil

Kernels from 1 medium ear of corn

3 garlic cloves, finely chopped

1 cup halved cherry tomatoes

1 small zucchini, cut into ½-inch pieces

8 ounces (16 pieces) large shrimp, peeled and deveined

Kosher salt

Freshly ground black pepper

Juice of 1 lemon

½ teaspoon extra-virgin olive oil (optional)

Per Serving: *Calories: 355; Fat: 11g; Carbohydrates: 37g; Fiber: 6g; Sugar: 10g; Protein: 32g; Sodium: 307mg*

1. Preheat the oven to 375°F. Line a baking sheet with parchment paper.
2. To make the croutons, spread out the bread in a single layer on the prepared baking sheet. Bake for 10 to 12 minutes, turning halfway through, until golden brown. Remove from the oven.
3. Meanwhile, heat a medium skillet over medium heat. Put the oil, corn, and garlic in the skillet, and cook for 1 minute, just until fragrant. Stir in the tomatoes and zucchini, and cook, stirring occasionally, for 3 minutes, until crisp-tender. Transfer to a plate.
4. Season the shrimp with salt and pepper, then add to the skillet. Cook, stirring occasionally, for 2 minutes, until opaque and cooked through. Return the vegetables to the skillet, and stir to combine.
5. Sprinkle with the lemon juice, and season with more salt and pepper if desired. Remove from the heat.
6. Divide the croutons evenly between 2 bowls. Top with the shrimp, and drizzle with the extra-virgin olive oil (if using).

PAIRS WELL WITH: This recipe feels like summer, and a crisp sauvignon blanc goes perfectly with it.

Sheet Pan Shrimp Bowls

SERVES 2 / PREP TIME: 15 MINUTES / COOK TIME: 15 MINUTES

My friend Stacey inspired this dish. She makes sheet pan meals to clean out her produce drawer and up her vegetable intake. This recipe includes a homemade ranch dressing to add some extra zing. You can replace the eggplant with potatoes, broccoli, celery, or squash, or add any additional vegetables you like, such as tomatoes. To make this recipe even easier, purchase frozen shrimp, and thaw only what you need before assembling.

FOR THE SHRIMP AND VEGETABLES

2 medium carrots, sliced (about 1 cup)

½ cup diced yellow onion

1 cup diced eggplant

1 tablespoon extra-virgin olive oil

Kosher salt

Freshly ground black pepper

8 ounces (10 to 12 pieces) fresh or frozen medium shrimp, peeled and deveined (thawed if frozen)

1 cup sliced white mushrooms

1 (10-ounce) package frozen brown rice

1. Preheat the oven to 425°F. Line a baking sheet with parchment paper.

2. **MAKE THE SHRIMP AND VEGETABLES:** Put the carrots, onion, and eggplant on the prepared baking sheet. Drizzle with the oil, and season with salt and pepper. Using tongs, toss until well coated. Arrange in even rows (leave some space for the shrimp and mushrooms). Bake for 10 minutes.

3. Meanwhile, season the shrimp on both sides with salt and pepper.

4. Remove the baking sheet from the oven. Using tongs, toss the vegetables. Add the shrimp and mushrooms, return to the oven, and bake for another 4 minutes, until opaque and cooked through. Remove from the oven.

5. **MAKE THE RANCH DRESSING:** In a small bowl, combine the yogurt, garlic, water, lemon juice, basil, and pepper. Whisk until smooth.

CONTINUED »

FOR THE RANCH DRESSING

⅓ cup full-fat plain Greek yogurt

1 garlic clove, minced

3 tablespoons water

1 tablespoon freshly squeezed lemon juice

1 teaspoon dried basil

Pinch freshly ground black pepper

Per Serving: *Calories: 413; Fat: 12g; Carbohydrates: 47g; Fiber: 6g; Sugar: 8g; Protein: 33g; Sodium: 761mg*

6. Heat the rice according to the package instructions.
7. Divide the rice evenly between 2 bowls. Top with the shrimp and roasted vegetables. Drizzle with the ranch dressing.

MAKE IT EASIER: You can also use your favorite store-bought dressing or sauce. Look for an all-natural brand without artificial ingredients or flavors.

USE IT UP: Leftover eggplant can be used in Beef Lettuce Wraps (page 122).

Teriyaki Shrimp and Veggie Bowls

SERVES 2 / PREP TIME: 5 MINUTES / COOK TIME: 10 MINUTES

This easy skillet meal is packed with fruits and vegetables. Bags of frozen cauliflower rice make this recipe a breeze, and folding in spinach bumps up the nutrients even more. Look for a teriyaki sauce without artificial colors or flavors. (I like P.F. Chang's, which can be found in most grocery stores.)

8 ounces (16 pieces) large shrimp, deveined and tails on

Kosher salt

Freshly ground black pepper

2 teaspoons avocado oil, divided

1 red bell pepper, seeded and sliced

½ small yellow onion, sliced

1 (10-ounce) bag frozen cauliflower rice

1 cup fresh or canned pineapple chunks

1 cup packed spinach

2 tablespoons teriyaki sauce

Per Serving: *Calories: 313; Fat: 6g; Carbohydrates: 41g; Fiber: 5g; Sugar: 16g; Protein: 28g; Sodium: 873mg*

1. Using a paper towel, pat dry the shrimp, then season each side with a pinch of salt and black pepper.
2. In a medium skillet, heat 1 teaspoon of oil over medium heat until it shimmers. Add the shrimp, and cook for 1 minute on each side. Transfer to a plate.
3. In the same skillet, heat the remaining 1 teaspoon of oil until it shimmers. Add the bell pepper and onion, and cook, stirring frequently, for 3 minutes, until softened.
4. Meanwhile, heat the cauliflower rice according to the package instructions.
5. Add the pineapple to the bell pepper mixture. Cook, stirring frequently, for 1 minute, until heated through. Remove from the heat.
6. Return the shrimp to the skillet, and toss to combine.
7. When the cauliflower is done, fold in the spinach, and stir until it is wilted.
8. Divide the cauliflower rice evenly between 2 bowls. Top with the shrimp and vegetables. Drizzle with the teriyaki sauce.

MAKE IT EASIER: Skip the knife work by using precut fresh vegetables (found in the produce department) or a frozen stir-fry mix.

Pesto Shrimp Pasta

SERVES 2 / PREP TIME: 10 MINUTES / COOK TIME: 10 MINUTES

I have been making a version of this pesto pasta at healthy cooking demonstrations for years. It's a fun and easy way to eat more greens. The flavors really come together thanks to a bit of freshly squeezed lemon juice. Look for a high-protein pasta (I like the Barilla Protein+ line). Frozen shrimp is ideal for this recipe because you can use the exact amount you want to eat.

1 cup dried high-protein penne

2½ cups spinach

½ cup fresh basil leaves

Zest of ½ lemon

⅓ cup walnut pieces

1 garlic clove

¼ cup freshly grated Parmesan cheese

1 tablespoon extra-virgin olive oil

1 tablespoon freshly squeezed lemon juice

⅛ teaspoon kosher salt

½ teaspoon freshly ground black pepper, plus more as needed

Nonstick cooking spray, for coating the skillet

8 ounces (16 pieces) fresh or frozen large shrimp, deveined and tails on (thawed if frozen)

Per Serving: *Calories: 510; Fat: 24g; Carbohydrates: 40g; Fiber: 4g; Sugar: 2g; Protein: 37g; Sodium: 483mg*

1. Bring a medium pot of water to a boil over high heat. Add the penne, and cook to al dente according to the package instructions. Remove from the heat. Drain, reserving ½ cup of the pasta cooking water, and return to the pot.

2. To make the pesto, in a food processor or small blender, combine the spinach, basil, lemon zest, walnuts, and garlic. Pulse 10 to 15 times, until finely chopped. Add the cheese, oil, lemon juice, salt, and pepper. Pulse to combine, scraping down the sides of the bowl as needed. If the pesto seems too thick, add the reserved pasta cooking water, 1 teaspoon at a time, until you achieve the desired consistency.

3. Add the pesto to the pot with the warm penne, and toss until well coated.

4. Heat a large skillet over medium heat. Spray with cooking spray. Season the shrimp with pepper, then add to the skillet. Cook for 1 to 1½ minutes on each side, until opaque and cooked through. Remove from the heat.

5. Add the shrimp to the pesto pasta, and gently toss to incorporate. Serve.

PAIRS WELL WITH: For extra flavor, add 1 cup halved cherry tomatoes.

Lobster Tails with Corn on the Cob

SERVES 2 / PREP TIME: 10 MINUTES / COOK TIME: 30 MINUTES

Lobster takes less than 10 minutes to broil to perfection. All you need for flavor is a little butter, but you can also season it with salt, pepper, paprika, or lemon juice.

2 ears of corn, shucked

2 (6- to 8-ounce) lobster tails

1 teaspoon butter

2 cups fresh or frozen broccoli florets

1 tablespoon extra-virgin olive oil

Kosher salt

Freshly ground black pepper

1. Position one oven rack about 7 inches from the broiler and another rack in the center. Preheat the broiler to high.

2. Wrap the corn in aluminum foil. Place the wrapped corn directly on the lower oven rack, and broil for 20 minutes, turning halfway through.

3. Meanwhile, line a baking sheet with aluminum foil. Place the lobster tails on one side of the prepared sheet. Using kitchen scissors, cut the center of each shell from the open end to the tail end. Gently open the shells slightly. Place ½ teaspoon of butter inside the slit of each lobster tail.

4. Put the broccoli on the other side of the baking sheet. Sprinkle with the oil and a pinch each of salt and pepper. Using tongs, toss until well coated. Spread out the broccoli in an even layer.

5. After the corn has cooked for 20 minutes, place the baking sheet on the higher oven rack. Broil for 6 to 7 minutes, until the lobster shells are lightly browned and the meat is opaque. Toss the broccoli halfway through to prevent burning.

Per Serving: *Calories: 307; Fat: 12g; Carbohydrates: 33g; Fiber: 5g; Sugar: 11g; Protein: 23g; Sodium: 542mg*

6. Remove the lobster and corn from the oven, and let cool for about 2 minutes, until easy to handle.

7. Using your hands, remove the lobster tails from their shells. Serve with the broccoli and corn.

SWAP OR SUBSTITUTE: You can also make this meal more substantial by including a side of rice or toasted bread.

Baked Tilapia Tacos

SERVES 2 / PREP TIME: 10 MINUTES / COOK TIME: 10 MINUTES

Fish tacos couldn't be easier than this baked version. The crispy cabbage and juicy peach ensure your meal is well rounded in textures, flavors, and nutrition. Look for blackening seasoning with the other seasoning blends at the grocery store, or use your favorite fish seasoning instead.

2 cups packed finely chopped green cabbage

Juice of ½ lime

Nonstick cooking spray, for coating

2 (5- to 6-ounce) tilapia fillets

1 tablespoon blackening seasoning

4 taco-size whole-wheat or corn tortillas

¼ cup full-fat sour cream

1 peach, pitted and thinly sliced

½ lime, cut into 4 wedges

Per Serving: *Calories: 487; Fat: 15g; Carbohydrates: 57g; Fiber: 11g; Sugar: 12g; Protein: 36g; Sodium: 525mg*

1. In a medium bowl, toss the cabbage with the lime juice.
2. Position an oven rack about 7 inches from the broiler. Preheat the broiler to high. Line a baking sheet with aluminum foil, and spray with cooking spray.
3. Put the tilapia fillets on the prepared baking sheet, and sprinkle both sides with the blackening seasoning. Broil for 7 to 8 minutes, or until the internal temperature reaches a minimum of 145°F and the fish flakes easily with a fork. Remove from the oven.
4. Layer each tortilla with 1 tablespoon of sour cream, ½ tilapia fillet, 4 peach slices, and ½ cup of cabbage. Serve each taco with a lime wedge.

SWAP OR SUBSTITUTE: You can substitute any thin white fish for tilapia. If you don't have access to peaches, use mango. To make these gluten-free, use a gluten-free corn tortilla.

Mahi Sandwich with Tangy Slaw

SERVES 2 / PREP TIME: 10 MINUTES / COOK TIME: 10 MINUTES

Mahi-mahi is a thick white fish with a mild flavor. It's a great place to start if you are trying to eat more seafood. This satisfying sandwich is made from one fillet cut in half. If you have a bigger appetite, make one fillet per person. Look for broccoli slaw with the precut vegetables. If you can't find it, use a coleslaw blend.

1 tablespoon avocado oil

1 (6- to 8-ounce) mahi-mahi fillet, skin removed

Kosher salt

Freshly ground black pepper

½ ripe Hass avocado, pitted and peeled

½ teaspoon sriracha, or to taste

2 medium whole-grain hamburger buns, like Dave's Killer Bread Burger Buns

1 plum tomato, thinly sliced

¼ cup full-fat plain Greek yogurt

1 teaspoon freshly squeezed lime juice

¼ cup pineapple tidbits, drained

1 tablespoon honey mustard

2 cups store-bought broccoli slaw

Per Serving: *Calories: 431; Fat: 19g; Carbohydrates: 37g; Fiber: 8g; Sugar: 12g; Protein: 21g; Sodium: 514mg*

1. In a medium skillet, heat the oil over medium-high heat until it shimmers.
2. While the pan heats, using a sharp knife, cut the mahi-mahi fillet in half, then pat dry using paper towels. Season both sides with salt and pepper.
3. Add the fillet to the skillet, and sear on each side for 2 to 3 minutes, until the fish is opaque and flakes easily with a fork. Remove form the heat.
4. Meanwhile, in a small bowl, using a fork, mash the avocado. Add the sriracha, and stir until well combined.
5. Toast the hamburger buns if desired. Smear both sides with half of the avocado mixture. Top one half of each bun with 2 tomato slices. On the other half, place the mahi-mahi fillet.
6. In a medium bowl, combine the yogurt, lime juice, pineapple, and mustard, then fold in the broccoli slaw and stir well. Serve the slaw alongside the sandwiches.

USE IT UP: You can also use full-fat Greek yogurt in the Sheet Pan Shrimp Bowls (page 59). Save any extra buns for Spicy Chicken Sandwiches (page 82).

Crispy Cod with Roasted Potatoes

SERVES 2 / PREP TIME: 10 MINUTES / COOK TIME: 20 MINUTES

Fish and chips is an iconic meal, but it can be time-consuming to make and greasy at a restaurant. This version is lighter and quicker. Cod is a buttery, delicate fish that's great for seafood newbies.

2 medium (3- to 4-inch) red potatoes, cut into wedges

1 teaspoon avocado oil, plus 1 tablespoon

½ teaspoon smoked paprika

⅛ teaspoon kosher salt

¼ teaspoon ground cumin

¼ teaspoon freshly ground black pepper

¼ teaspoon onion powder

2 (5- to 6-ounce) cod fillets

¾ cup plain panko bread crumbs

2 tablespoons mayonnaise

1 tablespoon Dijon mustard

1. Preheat the oven to 450°F. Line a baking sheet with parchment paper.

2. Put the potatoes on the prepared baking sheet, and drizzle with 1 teaspoon of oil.

3. In a small bowl, combine the smoked paprika, salt, cumin, pepper, and onion powder. Sprinkle over the potatoes. Using tongs, toss until well coated. Spread out the potatoes in a single layer. Roast for 20 minutes, flipping halfway through, until golden brown and tender. Remove from the oven.

4. Meanwhile, using paper towels, pat dry the cod fillets. Pour the bread crumbs onto a shallow plate. In a small bowl, whisk together the mayonnaise and mustard. Coat or brush both sides of the fillets with the mustard mixture. Dredge in the bread crumbs until completely covered.

5. In a medium skillet, heat the remaining 1 tablespoon of oil over medium heat until it shimmers. Add the fillets, and cook for 3 to 4 minutes on each side, until the outside is browned and the fish is opaque and flakes easily with a fork. Remove from the heat.

Per Serving: *Calories: 604; Fat: 23g; Carbohydrates: 66g; Fiber: 6g; Sugar: 6g; Protein: 35g; Sodium: 919mg*

6. Divide the roasted potato wedges evenly between 2 plates, and serve the cod fillets alongside.

PAIRS WELL WITH: Serve with a simple green salad or a Caesar salad on the side.

USE IT UP: Smoked paprika is used throughout this book in recipes like Pick-Your-Flavor Bean Burger (page 37), Quick Weeknight Gumbo (page 100), and Barbecued Salmon and Garlic Green Beans (page 78).

Seared Fish with Tomatoes and Spaghetti Squash

SERVES 2 / PREP TIME: 5 MINUTES / COOK TIME: 15 MINUTES

This delicious recipe relies on two time-saving hacks: canned tomatoes and frozen spaghetti squash. Canned and frozen vegetables make meals easy and nutritious. If you don't have any red wine, you can omit it, but it does give the sauce a nice depth.

2 (3- to 4-ounce) thin white fish fillets (flounder or tilapia)

Kosher salt

Freshly ground black pepper

Nonstick cooking spray, for coating the skillet

1 tablespoon avocado oil

3 garlic cloves, finely chopped

1 (14.5-ounce) can no-salt-added diced tomatoes, juices drained by half

¼ cup dry red wine, like merlot or cabernet sauvignon

1 tablespoon dried basil

1 (10-ounce) bag frozen spaghetti squash

1. Heat a large skillet over medium-high heat.
2. Season both sides of the fish fillets with salt and pepper.
3. Spray the skillet with cooking spray. Add the fillets, and sear for 1 to 2 minutes on each side, until the fish is opaque and flakes easily with a fork. Transfer to a plate.
4. Reduce the heat to medium. Add the oil and garlic and cook, stirring frequently, for about 30 seconds, until fragrant.
5. Stir in the tomatoes and their juices, wine, basil, ¼ teaspoon of salt, and ⅛ teaspoon of pepper. Cook, stirring occasionally, for 5 to 6 minutes, until the sauce has thickened.
6. Return the fillets to the skillet. Spoon some of the tomato sauce over the fillets (it's okay if the fillets break apart). Remove from the heat.
7. Prepare the spaghetti squash according to the package instructions. Using a fork, break it into shreds if needed.

Per Serving: *Calories: 238; Fat: 8g; Carbohydrates: 14g; Fiber: 4g; Sugar: 6g; Protein: 24g; Sodium: 457mg*

8. Divide the spaghetti squash evenly between 2 plates. Top each with a fish fillet and the tomato sauce.

SWAP OR SUBSTITUTE: You can use crushed tomatoes instead of diced for a smoother sauce. To prepare with fresh spaghetti squash instead of frozen, cut the spaghetti squash in half lengthwise. Place, cut-side down, in a 9-by-13-inch pan. Add ½ cup water to the pan. Bake at 375°F for 35 to 40 minutes, until tender. Let cool slightly before shredding into strands using a fork.

Tuna Cakes with Apricot Dipping Sauce

SERVES 2 / PREP TIME: 5 MINUTES / COOK TIME: 10 MINUTES

With a few fresh ingredients you can turn a simple, single serve pouch of tuna into a delicious meal in minutes. These tuna cakes include zucchini, but you can bulk up your meal by serving them on top of fresh greens or with a side of steamed vegetables.

FOR THE TUNA CAKES

1 (3-ounce) pouch albacore tuna, packed in water

2 large eggs

3 tablespoons plain panko bread crumbs

1 small zucchini, shredded (about 1 cup)

2 scallions, finely diced (about 2 tablespoons)

¼ teaspoon kosher salt

¼ teaspoon freshly ground black pepper

⅛ teaspoon ground ginger

1 tablespoon avocado oil

FOR THE DIPPING SAUCE

3 tablespoons apricot preserves

2 teaspoons white-wine vinegar

Per Serving: *Calories: 283; Fat: 12g; Carbohydrates: 30g; Fiber: 2g; Sugar: 14g; Protein: 17g; Sodium: 577mg*

1. **MAKE THE TUNA CAKES:** In a medium bowl, use a spatula to break the tuna into small chunks. Stir in the eggs and bread crumbs.
2. Roll the shredded zucchini into a double layer of paper towels, and squeeze out any excess water. Add to the bowl, and mix well. Add the scallions, salt, pepper, and ground ginger. Mix until well combined.
3. In a large skillet, heat the oil over medium heat until it shimmers.
4. Using your hands, shape about ¼ cup of the tuna mixture into a patty. Repeat with the remaining mixture. You should have 4 tuna cakes total.
5. Carefully place the tuna cakes in the hot oil, and cook for 4 minutes on each side, until golden brown. Remove from the heat.
6. **MAKE THE DIPPING SAUCE:** Meanwhile, in a small bowl, mix together the apricot preserves and vinegar. Serve alongside the tuna cakes for dipping.

USE IT UP: If you used a whole can of tuna instead of a pouch, save the extra for a salad or to top toast for lunch tomorrow.

Cornmeal-Crusted Flounder with Zucchini

SERVES 2 / PREP TIME: 5 MINUTES / COOK TIME: 10 MINUTES

Cornmeal gives this pan-fried flounder a crispy crust and makes it feel deep-fried. Paprika and chile powder add zip. For the spice blend, I prefer Montreal Chicken or Steak Seasoning (McCormick Grill Mates), but you can also use a blend of ½ teaspoon of salt and ¼ teaspoon of pepper.

2 (3- to 5-ounce) flounder fillets

Kosher salt

Freshly ground black pepper

¼ cup yellow cornmeal

½ teaspoon smoked paprika

½ teaspoon chipotle chile powder

1 tablespoon avocado oil

2 teaspoons extra-virgin olive oil

¾ teaspoon spice blend

1 medium zucchini, cut into ½-inch-thick half-moons

Per Serving: *Calories: 269; Fat: 15g; Carbohydrates: 14g; Fiber: 2g; Sugar: 1g; Protein: 20g; Sodium: 964mg*

1. Using paper towels, pat dry the flounder fillets. Season both sides with salt and pepper.
2. In a shallow dish, combine the cornmeal, paprika, and chile powder. Dredge the fillets in the mixture until evenly coated all over.
3. In a medium skillet, heat the avocado oil over medium heat until it shimmers. Add the fillets, and cook for 2 minutes on each side, or until the fish is opaque and flakes easily with a fork. Transfer to a plate.
4. Meanwhile, in a bowl, whisk together the olive oil and spice blend. Add the zucchini, and stir until well coated.
5. Add the zucchini to the skillet, and cook, stirring frequently, for 3 minutes, until slightly browned and softened. Remove from the heat.
6. Divide the flounder fillets and zucchini evenly between 2 plates.

SWAP OR SUBSTITUTE: Swap another firm fish like tilapia, cod, or grouper for the flounder.

Easy Salmon Sushi

SERVES 2 / PREP TIME: 15 MINUTES / COOK TIME: 15 MINUTES

It's fairly quick and easy to make homemade sushi. Although the cook time may look intensive, it's about the same as delivery—and this is definitely cheaper. I like using short-grain brown rice because it is a whole grain, has a sticky texture, and is cheaper than sushi rice. If you can't find it, use a true white sushi rice. A bamboo rolling mat is helpful but not necessary since you can use parchment paper instead. If you have any leftover salmon from another recipe, you can use it here instead of smoked salmon.

½ cup sushi rice, rinsed and drained

¾ cup water

1 tablespoon rice vinegar

2 sheets nori seaweed

2 ounces smoked salmon

1 medium carrot, shredded (about ¼ cup)

1 mini seedless cucumber, julienned

½ Hass avocado, pitted, peeled, and sliced

12 ounces frozen whole-pod edamame

1. In a small pot, combine the rice and water, and bring to a boil over medium-high heat. Reduce the heat to medium-low, cover, and simmer for about 15 minutes, until the rice is tender and has absorbed most of the liquid. Immediately remove the rice from the pot and spread it over a large plate or baking sheet to cool until ready to assemble. Sprinkle the cooked rice with the vinegar.

2. Lay out 1 square foot of parchment paper on a cutting board. Place a sheet of nori on top.

3. Set up a small bowl of water. Wet your fingertips, and spread ¾ cup of the cooked rice in a thin layer on the nori sheet, leaving a ½-inch space at the top edge. Be sure to spread the rice to both sides.

4. Lay 1 ounce of the salmon along the bottom edge of the rice. Spread 2 tablespoons of shredded carrot on top of the salmon. Top with 2 to 4 cucumber sticks and 2 or 3 avocado slices.

Per Serving: *Calories: 579; Fat: 19g; Carbohydrates: 62g; Fiber: 13g; Sugar: 7g; Protein: 46g; Sodium: 297mg*

5. Roll the sushi: Starting at the longest edge closest to you, lift the parchment paper and roll the sushi onto itself one time, about half-way up. Through the parchment paper, gently squeeze the roll to tighten. Lift the parchment paper, and roll the nori again to close on itself. Gently squeeze a second time through the parchment paper to tightly seal.

6. Using a clean, sharp knife, cut the sushi roll in half, then cut each in half again. Cut each quarter so you end up with 8 pieces of sushi. Repeat with the remaining nori sheet, cooked rice, salmon, carrot, cucumber, and avocado.

7. Meanwhile, heat the edamame according to the package instructions. Divide the sushi rolls evenly between 2 plates, and serve the edamame alongside.

MAKE IT EASIER: If you own a rice cooker or an electric pressure cooker, use it to save time and avoid worrying about whether the rice is done. You can also buy sushi rice from a restaurant, which is an easy way to get started with making sushi at home.

Simple Salmon Packets with Sweet Potatoes

SERVES 2 / PREP TIME: 10 MINUTES / COOK TIME: 25 MINUTES

If you want juicy fish, a foolproof method is baking it in parchment packets. Don't worry about making a perfect envelope; just get it tight enough to hold in the steam. Herbes de Provence is a light all-in-one seasoning blend. If you don't have it on hand, substitute dried thyme or even just salt and pepper.

2 medium sweet potatoes, peeled and cut into ½-inch dice

3 teaspoons extra-virgin olive oil, divided

2 teaspoons herbes de Provence, divided

2 (4- to 5-ounce) skin-on salmon fillets

Kosher salt

Freshly ground black pepper

1 lemon, thinly sliced

1. Preheat the oven to 425°F. Line a baking sheet with aluminum foil.

2. Put the sweet potatoes on the prepared baking sheet. Drizzle with 2 teaspoons of oil, and sprinkle with 1 teaspoon of herbes de Provence. Using tongs, toss until well coated. Spread out the sweet potatoes in a single layer on one side of the baking sheet. Bake for 10 minutes.

3. Meanwhile, lay out two 12-by-12-inch sheets of parchment paper. Place one salmon fillet on the bottom half of each piece of parchment. Drizzle each salmon fillet with ½ teaspoon of oil, and season each with ½ teaspoon of herbes de Provence and a pinch each of salt and pepper. Cover each with 3 lemon slices.

4. To make each packet, fold the top half of the parchment paper over the fillet. Tightly roll the bottom edge, pressing with each fold. Repeat with the 2 short sides to seal the fillet (it's okay if the edges unravel a little).

Per Serving: *Calories: 344; Fat: 14g; Carbohydrates: 29g; Fiber: 5g; Sugar: 6g; Protein: 25g; Sodium: 415mg*

5. Once the sweet potatoes have baked for 10 minutes, remove the baking sheet from the oven, and reduce the temperature to 375°F.

6. Place the salmon packets on the other side of the baking sheet. Using tongs, toss the sweet potatoes, then return the baking sheet to the oven. Cook for another 15 minutes, until the sweet potatoes are tender and browned and the fish flakes easily with a fork.

7. Remove from the oven, and let sit for 1 to 2 minutes. Carefully break open the parchment packets, and transfer the salmon fillets to 2 plates. Serve with the sweet potatoes on the side.

SWAP OR SUBSTITUTE: You can cook almost any type of fish in a foil packet. Thinner fish like tilapia may need less baking time.

Barbecued Salmon and Garlic Green Beans

SERVES 2 / PREP TIME: 10 MINUTES / COOK TIME: 15 MINUTES

If you're not totally sold on salmon but are trying to like it, start with this recipe. You can certainly use your favorite store-bought barbecue sauce, but this homemade version uses pantry staples and has less sodium and sugar.

FOR THE BARBECUE SAUCE

1 tablespoon tomato paste

1 tablespoon liquid honey

1 teaspoon smoked paprika

1 teaspoon apple cider vinegar

1 teaspoon Worcestershire sauce

FOR THE SALMON AND GREEN BEANS

2 (4-ounce) skin-on salmon fillets

Kosher salt

Freshly ground black pepper

2 cups green beans

2 teaspoons extra-virgin olive oil

2 teaspoons garlic powder

Per Serving: Calories: 275; Fat: 10g; Carbohydrates: 21g; Fiber: 4g; Sugar: 13g; Protein: 28g; Sodium: 208mg

1. Preheat the oven to 400°F. Line a baking sheet with aluminum foil.

2. **MAKE THE BARBECUE SAUCE:** In a small bowl, whisk together the tomato paste, honey, paprika, vinegar, and Worcestershire sauce.

3. **MAKE THE SALMON AND GREEN BEANS:** Place the salmon fillets on one side of the prepared baking sheet. Sprinkle with a pinch each of salt and pepper. Cover with the barbecue sauce.

4. Place the green beans on the other side of the baking sheet. Drizzle with the oil, and sprinkle with the garlic powder. Using tongs, toss until well coated.

5. Bake for 10 to 12 minutes, or until the internal temperature of the fish reaches 145°F and it flakes easily with a fork (if using coho salmon, the cook time may be shorter). Remove from the oven.

6. Divide the salmon and green beans evenly between 2 plates.

SWAP OR SUBSTITUTE: Swap in asparagus, broccoli, or cauliflower for the green beans.

Mom's 10-Minute Salmon with Charred Brussels Sprouts

SERVES 2 / PREP TIME: 10 MINUTES / COOK TIME: 10 MINUTES

My mom makes broiled salmon once a week for herself and my dad. I've heard about it so much that I had to try it, too. I tweaked the dish to make it easier to prepare, including cooking the vegetables in the same pan. This meal is gluten-free and low in carbs.

1½ cups Brussels sprouts, cut in half

1 tablespoon extra-virgin olive oil

Kosher salt

Freshly ground black pepper

2 (4-ounce) skin-on salmon fillets

1½ teaspoons butter, melted

2 teaspoons brown sugar

Per Serving: *Calories: 275; Fat: 15g; Carbohydrates: 10g; Fiber: 2g; Sugar: 6g; Protein: 27g; Sodium: 181mg*

1. Position an oven rack about 7 inches from the broiler. Preheat the broiler to high. Line a baking sheet with aluminum foil.

2. On one side of the prepared baking sheet, place the Brussels sprouts. Drizzle with oil, then season with salt and pepper. Using tongs, toss until well coated. Place the salmon fillets, skin-side down, on the other side of the baking sheet, and season with salt and pepper. Brush each fillet with the butter, then sprinkle with 1 teaspoon of brown sugar, spreading evenly.

3. Broil for 7 to 8 minutes, or until the fish is opaque and flakes easily with a fork and the Brussels sprouts are charred.

4. Remove from the oven, and let rest for 2 to 3 minutes. Using a slotted spatula, lift the salmon off its skin, which should stick to the foil, and place on 2 plates. Divide the Brussels sprouts evenly on the side.

PAIRS WELL WITH: If you want to add a bit more sustenance, serve with ½ cup brown rice per person or a slice of crusty bread.

Chapter 5
Poultry

Spicy Chicken Sandwiches

SERVES 2 / PREP TIME: 10 MINUTES / COOK TIME: 10 MINUTES

It's easy to hit the drive-through for a chicken sandwich, but you might think twice about it after trying this super simple homemade version. I like using whole-grain hamburger buns (Dave's Killer Bread Burger Buns taste amazing) for an extra dose of filling fiber.

1 large egg

1 teaspoon
2 percent milk

2 teaspoons
sriracha, divided

¼ cup cornmeal

1 tablespoon
all-purpose flour

⅛ teaspoon kosher salt

⅛ teaspoon freshly
ground black pepper

1 tablespoon avocado oil

2 (4-ounce)
chicken cutlets

2 whole-grain buns

½ Hass avocado, pitted
and peeled

2 lettuce leaves

2 thick tomato slices

Per Serving: *Calories: 505; Fat:
22g; Carbohydrates: 42g; Fiber:
6g; Sugar: 6g; Protein: 36g;
Sodium: 518mg*

1. Prepare a breading station: In one shallow dish, whisk together the egg, milk, and 1 teaspoon of sriracha. In another dish, combine the cornmeal, flour, salt, and pepper.
2. In a medium skillet, heat the oil over medium heat until it shimmers.
3. Dredge the chicken in the egg mixture, then coat completely in the cornmeal mixture. Add to the skillet, and cook for 3 minutes on each side, until golden brown or the internal temperature reaches 165°F. Remove from the heat.
4. Toast the buns if desired.
5. In a small bowl, using a fork, mash the avocado with the remaining 1 teaspoon of sriracha, and spread on both sides of the buns. On the bun bottoms, layer the chicken, lettuce, and tomato. Top with the bun tops.

PAIRS WELL WITH: Serve this sandwich with a garden salad (lettuce, tomato, cucumber) or additional steamed vegetables, like broccoli or your favorite frozen mix.

Chicken Tenders with Peanut Sauce

SERVES 2 / PREP TIME: 5 MINUTES / COOK TIME: 10 MINUTES

This recipe is a nod to chicken satay with peanut dipping sauce. It's super quick and easy, with a boost of vegetables thanks to the frozen blend. I like shredded cabbage and carrots, but you can swap in any veggie blend that suits you.

FOR THE PEANUT SAUCE

2 tablespoons natural creamy peanut butter

2 teaspoons reduced-sodium soy sauce

Juice of ½ lime

½ teaspoon hoisin sauce

2 tablespoons water

FOR THE CHICKEN TENDERS

1 teaspoon avocado oil

4 (2-ounce) chicken tenderloins

Kosher salt

Freshly ground black pepper

1 (10-ounce) package frozen shredded cabbage and carrots (I like Birds Eye)

⅓ cup chopped fresh cilantro leaves

2 tablespoons roasted unsalted peanuts, chopped

Per Serving: *Calories: 380; Fat: 18g; Carbohydrates: 23g; Fiber: 6g; Sugar: 11g; Protein: 33g; Sodium: 491mg*

1. **MAKE THE PEANUT SAUCE:** In a small bowl, whisk together the peanut butter, soy sauce, lime juice, hoisin, and water.

2. **MAKE THE CHICKEN TENDERS:** In a medium skillet, heat the oil over medium-high heat just until it shimmers.

3. Season the chicken on both sides with a pinch each of salt and pepper. Add to the skillet, and sear for 2 minutes on each side, or until cooked through and no longer pink inside. Transfer to a plate.

4. To the same skillet, add the cabbage and carrots, and cook, stirring frequently, for 5 minutes, until heated through. Remove from the heat.

5. Divide the vegetables evenly between 2 plates. Top with the chicken tenders. Sprinkle with the cilantro and peanuts. Serve the peanut sauce on the side or drizzled over the top.

PAIRS WELL WITH: To turn this recipe into a rice bowl, serve it over ½ cup white or brown rice per person.

Apricot Chicken with Spinach Rice

SERVES 2 / PREP TIME: 10 MINUTES / COOK TIME: 15 MINUTES

This chicken recipe has become my go-to for a satisfying weeknight meal. It tastes fancy and indulgent but couldn't be easier. Spinach is folded right into the warm rice to reduce the number of dishes. You can use any rice substitute, like couscous, cauliflower rice, or any other plant-based rice.

2 boneless, skinless chicken thighs

Kosher salt

Freshly ground black pepper

2 teaspoons avocado oil

1 (8.8-ounce) pouch microwavable brown or white rice

3 cups packed chopped spinach leaves

2 tablespoons water

2 tablespoons balsamic vinegar

⅓ cup apricot preserves

1. Heat a medium skillet with a lid over medium-high heat.

2. Season the chicken with a pinch each of salt and pepper.

3. Put the oil in the hot skillet. Add the chicken, cover, and cook, undisturbed, for 4 to 5 minutes. Flip the chicken, cover, and cook, undisturbed, for another 4 to 5 minutes. When the internal temperature reaches 160°F, remove from the heat. Transfer to a plate, and tent with aluminum foil to keep warm. Reduce the heat to medium low and return the skillet to the burner.

4. Meanwhile, prepare the rice according to the package instructions. Fold the spinach into the cooked rice.

Per Serving: *Calories: 510; Fat: 12g; Carbohydrates: 67g; Fiber: 3g; Sugar: 26g; Protein: 34g; Sodium: 358mg*

5. In the same skillet, combine the water and vinegar, and bring to a simmer over medium-low heat. Using a spoon, scrape up the browned bits from the bottom. Whisk in the apricot preserves until combined. Simmer for about 1 minute, until the sauce thickens slightly. Return the chicken to the skillet, and turn to coat in the sauce. Remove from the heat.

6. Divide the spinach rice evenly between 2 plates, and top with the chicken and sauce.

SWAP OR SUBSTITUTE: Chicken tenders and chicken cutlets can be substituted for thighs without significant changes to the cook time. You can use orange marmalade instead of apricot preserves.

Pineapple Chicken

SERVES 2 / PREP TIME: 10 MINUTES / COOK TIME: 10 MINUTES

Grilled pineapple and chicken kebabs are an iconic weekend meal that exudes relaxation and deliciousness. This recipe is a riff on that idea so you can enjoy the dish on a busy day. Pureeing the pineapple and peppers creates a delicious sauce with no added sugar. Adobo seasoning is a Latin spice blend that packs a lot of flavor. If you can't find it, substitute taco seasoning blend.

Nonstick cooking spray, for coating

1 (8-ounce) chicken breast, cut into 1-inch dice

1 teaspoon adobo seasoning

1 red bell pepper, cut into 1-inch chunks

1 green bell pepper, cut into 1-inch chunks

½ red onion, cut into ½-inch pieces

2 teaspoons extra-virgin olive oil

¼ teaspoon kosher salt

⅛ teaspoon freshly ground black pepper

1½ cups chopped pineapple (½-inch pieces)

½ cup instant white or brown rice or microwavable pouch rice

1. Position an oven rack 3 to 4 inches from the broiler. Preheat the broiler to high. Line a baking sheet with aluminum foil, and spray with cooking spray.

2. On one side of the prepared baking sheet, using tongs, toss the chicken with the adobo seasoning. On the other side of the baking sheet, using tongs, toss the red bell pepper, green bell pepper, and onion with the oil, salt, and black pepper. Arrange the red peppers together so it's easier to collect them after cooking. Leave space for the pineapple.

3. Spread out the pineapple in the remaining space on the baking sheet. Broil for 3 to 5 minutes, until the internal temperature of the chicken reaches 160°F to 165°F.

4. Meanwhile, prepare the rice according to the package instructions.

Per Serving: *Calories: 282; Fat: 6g; Carbohydrates: 52g; Fiber: 5g; Sugar: 17g; Protein: 8g; Sodium: 784mg*

5. Remove from the oven, and set aside for 2 minutes. Transfer half of both the red peppers and pineapple to a blender or food processor. Carefully blend until smooth, allowing some of the steam to escape from the hole in the lid.

6. Divide the rice evenly between 2 bowls, and top with the chicken and vegetables. Drizzle with the pineapple puree.

PAIRS WELL WITH: If you want even more vegetables in this meal, simply add your favorites to the pan when roasting.

USE IT UP: Adobo seasoning is also used in the Adobo Turkey Nachos (page 101) and you can also use up the extra onion in this recipe, too.

Mediterranean-Style Chicken Bowls

SERVES 2 / PREP TIME: 10 MINUTES / COOK TIME: 10 MINUTES

This is my homage to a chicken bowl from a popular Mediterranean restaurant. If you've never tried cauliflower rice, this is a great recipe to start with—you may not even notice a difference. If you'd like some extra flavor, drizzle the cauliflower rice with about 1 teaspoon of Greek-style vinaigrette after heating.

FOR THE GARLIC YOGURT SAUCE

½ cup full-fat plain Greek yogurt

2 teaspoons freshly squeezed lemon juice

1 garlic clove, minced

½ teaspoon dried dill

FOR THE CHICKEN BOWL

4 (2-ounce) chicken tenderloins

½ teaspoon kosher salt

½ teaspoon freshly ground black pepper

1 teaspoon avocado oil

1 (10-ounce) package frozen cauliflower rice

½ cup diced cucumber

½ cup shredded or matchstick carrots

⅓ cup pitted Kalamata olives

¼ cup crumbled feta cheese

1. **MAKE THE GARLIC YOGURT SAUCE:** In a small bowl, combine the yogurt, lemon juice, garlic, and dill. Mix well.

2. **MAKE THE CHICKEN BOWL:** Season the chicken on both sides with the salt and pepper. In a medium skillet, heat the oil over medium-high heat until it shimmers. Add the chicken, and cook for 3 minutes on each side, until the internal temperature reaches about 165°F. Remove from the heat. Let cool for about 2 minutes, then slice the chicken into thin strips.

3. Meanwhile, prepare the cauliflower rice according to the package instructions.

4. Divide the cauliflower rice evenly between 2 bowls. Top with the chicken, cucumber, carrots, olives, cheese, and yogurt sauce.

SWAP OR SUBSTITUTE: Make this bowl vegetarian by substituting an equal amount of canned chickpeas or tempeh in place of the chicken and using a vegetarian cheese. You can add regular rice here in place of or in addition to the cauliflower rice.

Per Serving: *Calories: 357; Fat: 16g; Carbohydrates: 17g; Fiber: 5g; Sugar: 9g; Protein: 38g; Sodium: 1,051mg*

Chicken Enchilada Casserole

SERVES 2 / PREP TIME: 10 MINUTES / COOK TIME: 20 MINUTES

Casseroles aren't typically made for a group of two, but that's about to change. You can find individual square ramekins easily online, and they make the perfect vessel for this dish. The recipe easily doubles to feed four or freeze for later. You can also swap in your favorite salsa (I recommend a non-chunky brand) for the salsa verde.

Nonstick cooking spray, for coating the ramekins

1 chicken breast, cut into bite-size pieces

¼ cup diced onion

1 medium green bell pepper, seeded and diced (about ¼ cup)

2 (8-inch) whole-wheat tortillas, cut into bite-size pieces

1 cup packed chopped spinach

1 tablespoon plus 1 teaspoon all-purpose flour

¾ cup store-bought salsa verde

½ cup shredded Mexican-style cheese blend

Per Serving: *Calories: 467; Fat: 17g; Carbohydrates: 34g; Fiber: 8g; Sugar: 7g; Protein: 43g; Sodium: 920mg*

1. Preheat the oven to 400°F.
2. Spray 2 square ramekins (about 4½ inches by 4½ inches) with cooking spray.
3. In a medium bowl, combine the chicken, onion, bell pepper, tortillas, spinach, flour, and salsa verde. Mix well.
4. Dividing evenly, spoon the mixture into the prepared ramekins. Top each with ¼ cup of cheese.
5. Place the ramekins on a baking sheet. Bake for 20 minutes, until heated through and the cheese is melted.
6. Remove from the oven, and let rest for 5 minutes before serving.

USE IT UP: Use up the salsa verde in Chicken Salsa Verde Soup (page 21) or Black Bean-Stuffed Bell Peppers with Plantains (page 39).

Mango-Cashew Chicken with Sweet Peas

SERVES 2 / PREP TIME: 5 MINUTES / COOK TIME: 15 MINUTES

When dining out, I can never choose between mango chicken and cashew chicken, and that dilemma inspired this recipe. The sauce is light and creamy, and it coats the chicken beautifully. This recipe is a great foundation, but feel free to spice up the sauce with a pinch of ginger or add more vegetables or beans.

1 cup fresh or frozen chopped mango (thawed if frozen)

1 tablespoon avocado oil

2 boneless, skinless chicken thighs

Kosher salt

Freshly ground black pepper

½ cup light coconut milk

1½ cups frozen peas

⅓ cup unsalted roasted cashews

Per Serving: *Calories: 541; Fat: 28g; Carbohydrates: 35g; Fiber: 7g; Sugar: 18g; Protein: 39g; Sodium: 410mg*

1. In a blender, puree the mango until smooth.
2. In a medium skillet, heat the oil over medium-high heat until it shimmers.
3. Season both sides of the chicken with a pinch each of salt and pepper. Sear for about 4 minutes on each side, or until the internal temperature reaches a minimum of 160°F. Transfer to a plate.
4. Reduce the heat to low. In the same skillet, combine the coconut milk, mango puree, and peas. Cook, stirring continuously using a wooden spoon to pick up any browned bits on the bottom, for 2 to 3 minutes, until the sauce slightly thickens and the peas are warmed. Remove from the heat. Stir in the cashews, and return the chicken to the skillet. Mix to coat the chicken with sauce.
5. Divide the chicken and sauce evenly between 2 bowls.

PAIRS WELL WITH: To make this meal a little heartier, serve with rice, cauliflower rice, or naan.

Parmesan Chicken over Wild Rice

SERVES 2 / PREP TIME: 10 MINUTES / COOK TIME: 15 MINUTES

If you need to pull off a high-end-type meal on a busy weeknight, this recipe is just the ticket. It has all the makings of a classy dish, lightened up with a good dose of kale and mushrooms. You can swap in other cuts of chicken or even cut chicken breasts into strips.

1 large egg

1 tablespoon
2 percent milk

¼ cup plain
bread crumbs

¼ cup freshly grated
Parmesan cheese,
plus more for
garnish (optional)

1 tablespoon avocado oil

4 (2-ounce) chicken
tenderloins

Kosher salt

Freshly ground
black pepper

1 small onion or shallot,
diced (about ¼ cup)

½ cup dry white wine,
like chardonnay

½ cup reduced-sodium
chicken broth

1. Prepare a breading station: In one shallow dish, whisk together the egg and milk. In another shallow dish, combine the bread crumbs and ¼ cup of cheese.

2. In a medium skillet, heat the oil over medium heat until it shimmers. Season the chicken on both sides with a pinch each of salt and pepper. Dredge the chicken in the egg mixture, then coat both sides in the bread crumb mixture. Add to the skillet, and cook for 2 to 3 minutes on each side (it does not need to be cooked completely through). Transfer to a plate.

3. To the same skillet, add the onion, and sauté for 1 minute, until softened. Add the wine, broth, kale, and mushrooms. Cook, stirring with a wooden spoon to loosen the browned bits on the bottom, for 4 to 5 minutes, until the wine is reduced by half. Return the chicken to the skillet for the last 2 minutes of cooking, just to heat through. Remove from the heat, and tent with aluminum foil to keep warm.

1 cup finely chopped
kale leaves

1 cup sliced mushrooms
or 1 (6.5-ounce)
can mushroom
pieces, drained

1 (8.8-ounce) pouch
microwavable wild rice

Per Serving: *Calories: 562; Fat:
16g; Carbohydrates: 51g; Fiber:
2g; Sugar: 3g; Protein: 39g;
Sodium: 519mg*

4. Meanwhile, prepare the rice according to the
   package instructions.
5. Divide the rice evenly between 2 plates. Spoon
   the chicken and sauce over the rice, and sprinkle with more cheese (if using).

PAIRS WELL WITH: A glass of chardonnay is the
perfect complement to this meal.

USE IT UP: Kale can be used up in Sweet Potato,
Kale, and Egg Stacks (page 46) or Avocado-Kale
Salad with Seared Salmon (page 27).

Pizza-Stuffed Chicken with Mashed Cauliflower

SERVES 2 / PREP TIME: 10 MINUTES / COOK TIME: 15 MINUTES

I once asked my son for a new recipe idea, and he quickly replied "pizza chicken." The idea has never left me, and I finally got to create a quick chicken dinner that nods to the flavors of pizza.

2 boneless, skinless chicken breasts

½ teaspoon dried basil, plus ⅛ teaspoon

2 tablespoons tomato paste

2 ounces sliced fresh mozzarella cheese, divided into 1-ounce portions

8 turkey pepperoni slices

Kosher salt

Freshly ground black pepper

1 tablespoon avocado oil

3 cups frozen cauliflower rice

1 tablespoon salted butter

1. Preheat the oven to 375°F.

2. Place the chicken breasts between 2 pieces of parchment paper or plastic wrap. Using a kitchen mallet, gently pound to an equal thickness of ¼ inch to ½ inch.

3. Sprinkle one side of each flattened chicken breast with ¼ teaspoon of basil, then cover with 1 tablespoon of tomato paste. Top with 1 ounce of cheese and 4 pepperoni slices. Starting at the shorter edge, roll up the chicken tightly, securing it closed with a wooden toothpick. Season with a pinch each of salt and pepper.

4. In a medium oven-safe skillet, heat the oil over medium heat until it shimmers. Place the chicken rolls, seam-side down, in the skillet, and cook for 2 minutes. Carefully flip, and sear for another 2 minutes. Flip again, and bake for 8 to 9 minutes, until the internal temperature reaches 165°F. Remove from the oven.

Per Serving: *Calories: 573; Fat: 21g; Carbohydrates: 17g; Fiber: 7g; Sugar: 8g; Protein: 80g; Sodium: 630mg*

5. Meanwhile, to make the cauliflower mash, cook the cauliflower rice according to the package instructions. Spoon the rice into a blender, add the butter and pinch each of salt and pepper, and puree until smooth. Add the remaining ⅛ teaspoon of dried basil and pulse just to combine.

6. Serve the pizza-stuffed chicken alongside the cauliflower mash.

MAKE IT EASIER: If you use a thin chicken or turkey cutlet, you can skip the pounding.

Banh Mi–Style Sandwiches

SERVES 2 / PREP TIME: 15 MINUTES / COOK TIME: 5 MINUTES

Banh Mi is a Vietnamese-style sandwich typically filled with shredded meat, pickled vegetables, and cilantro—and it's a personal favorite of mine. This lightened-up version is quick and easy any time you have a hankering for a hot sandwich. I like using an olive oil–based mayonnaise, but you can skip it if you're not a mayo person.

1 cup shredded or matchstick carrots, divided

½ large cucumber, cut into thin coins

¼ cup rice vinegar, plus 1 tablespoon

Kosher salt

2 tablespoons hoisin sauce

2 chicken or turkey cutlets

1 (10- to 12-inch) whole-grain baguette, cut in half and sliced open

1 teaspoon avocado oil

2 tablespoons mayonnaise

⅓ cup chopped fresh cilantro leaves

2 cups packed mixed salad greens

1. In a shallow bowl, mix together the carrots, cucumber, ¼ cup of vinegar, and a pinch of salt. Set aside, and toss occasionally, keeping the vegetables covered by the vinegar as much as possible.

2. In a medium bowl, mix together the hoisin sauce and remaining 1 tablespoon of vinegar.

3. Using a sharp knife, thinly slice the cutlets against the grain into ½-inch strips. Place in the hoisin marinade, and let sit for 5 minutes.

4. Preheat the oven to 375°F. Put the baguette on a baking sheet, and bake for 5 minutes, just until toasted. Remove from the oven.

5. Meanwhile, in a medium skillet, heat the oil over medium-high heat until it shimmers. Add the chicken to the skillet. Cook, stirring occasionally, for about 3 minutes, until cooked through. Remove from the heat.

6. Assemble the sandwiches: Spread 1 tablespoon of mayonnaise on each toasted baguette. Add half of the chicken, one-quarter of the carrot and cucumber mixture, and one-quarter of the cilantro to each. Top each with the other half of the baguette.

Per Serving: *Calories: 444; Fat: 18g; Carbohydrates: 34g; Fiber: 4g; Sugar: 10g; Protein: 37g; Sodium: 744mg*

7. Divide the salad greens evenly between 2 plates. Top with the remaining carrot and cucumber mixture plus any additional cilantro, and serve alongside the sandwiches.

MAKE IT EASIER: If you like kimchi, swap out the quick-pickled carrots and cucumbers for store-bought kimchi. Dress the salad with your favorite salad dressing if desired.

Turkey-Cranberry Sandwiches with Green Beans

SERVES 2 / PREP TIME: 10 MINUTES / COOK TIME: 15 MINUTES

The flavors of Thanksgiving are too good to be enjoyed only once a year. Using quick-cooking extra-lean turkey cutlets enables you to get this well-balanced meal on the table in a matter of minutes. If you can't find whole-berry cranberry sauce, substitute a tart jelly.

¼ teaspoon kosher salt

1 tablespoon garlic powder

1 teaspoon dried rosemary

2 tablespoons avocado oil, divided

2 turkey breast cutlets

2 cups (or handfuls) green beans

Nonstick cooking spray, for coating the skillet

¼ cup water

½ cup whole-berry cranberry sauce

2 whole-grain sandwich rolls, halved

4 butter lettuce leaves

2 ounces goat cheese, softened

1. In a small bowl, combine the salt, garlic powder, rosemary, and 1 tablespoon of oil. Rub the mixture on both sides of the cutlets.

2. In a large mixing bowl, toss the green beans in the remaining 1 tablespoon of oil.

3. Heat a large skillet over medium heat, and spray with cooking spray. Add the turkey, and cook for 2 to 3 minutes on each side, until the internal temperature reaches 160°F. Transfer to a plate, and tent with aluminum foil to keep warm.

4. If needed, spray the skillet with cooking spray again. Add the green beans, and cook, stirring occasionally, for 4 minutes. Add the water, and cook for another 4 minutes, until crisp-tender. Remove from the heat.

Per Serving: *Calories: 563;*
Fat 23g; Carbohydrates:
59g; Fiber: 5g; Protein: 33g;
Sodium: 750mg

5. Assemble the sandwiches: Smear the cranberry sauce on the bottom half of each roll. Top each with the turkey and 2 lettuce leaves. Smear 1 ounce of goat cheese on the top half of each roll, and place on top of the lettuce.

6. Serve each sandwich with a side of green beans.

SWAP OR SUBSTITUTE: If you can't find butter lettuce, any type of lettuce will work here. If you want fewer carbohydrates in your meal, choose sandwich thins or lettuce wraps.

Quick Weeknight Gumbo

SERVES 2 / PREP TIME: 5 MINUTES / COOK TIME: 30 MINUTES

Meat-and-rice dishes can be so comforting. Here's a quick riff on slow-cooking gumbo. If your grocery store doesn't carry a frozen gumbo vegetable mix, look for one that includes okra, corn, celery, onions, and red bell peppers, or the closest thing you can find. You can also use canned vegetables.

1 teaspoon avocado oil

1 boneless, skinless chicken thigh

1 pinch plus ⅛ teaspoon kosher salt, divided

Freshly ground black pepper

1 cup reduced-sodium chicken broth

⅓ cup quick-cooking white or brown rice

4 ounces smoked turkey sausage, diced

1½ cups frozen gumbo vegetables

¼ teaspoon onion powder

¼ teaspoon smoked paprika

¼ teaspoon garlic powder

⅛ teaspoon ground cayenne pepper

Per Serving: *Calories: 545; Fat: 12g; Carbohydrates: 72g; Fiber: 10g; Sugar: 2g; Protein: 35g; Sodium: 1,298mg*

1. In a small Dutch oven or stockpot, heat the oil over medium-high heat until it shimmers. Season the chicken on both sides with a pinch of salt and pepper. Add to the pot, and cook for 3 to 4 minutes on each side, or until the internal temperature reaches 165°F.

2. Transfer the chicken to a cutting board, and shred or dice it.

3. Add the broth to the same pot, and bring to a boil over medium-high heat, using a wooden spoon to scrape up the browned bits from the bottom. Stir in the rice and sausage, and return the mixture to a boil. Reduce the heat to medium-low, cover, and simmer for 13 to 15 minutes, until the rice is tender and has absorbed most of the liquid.

4. Add the shredded chicken, vegetables, onion powder, paprika, garlic powder, cayenne pepper, and ⅛ teaspoon of salt. Stir to combine, then cover and cook for 5 minutes, just until the vegetables are heated through. Remove from the heat.

5. Divide the gumbo evenly between 2 bowls.

PAIRS WELL WITH: This gumbo has a little kick, so it pairs well with a grenache, a red wine also called garnacha, or a blend that includes it.

Adobo Turkey Nachos

SERVES 2 / PREP TIME: 5 MINUTES / COOK TIME: 15 MINUTES

Nachos can be a balanced meal when you include some extra vegetables. Adding broccoli slaw is a superfood hack that you can use in many other dishes, too, like Beef-Broccoli Stir-Fry (page 124). Sautéing the slaw with the turkey makes it more flavorful and tender. Adobo is a great all-in-one Latinx seasoning blend. You can find it in the spice aisle at your grocery store or online.

1 teaspoon avocado oil

¼ cup diced onion

1 cup store-bought broccoli slaw

8 ounces lean ground turkey

1 teaspoon adobo seasoning

2 servings tortilla chips

1 cup shredded cheese of choice

1 cup seeded and diced tomatoes

1 cup chopped lettuce

2 tablespoons full-fat sour cream (optional)

Per Serving: *Calories: 626; Fat: 40g; Carbohydrates: 30g; Fiber: 5g; Sugar: 5g; Protein: 39g; Sodium: 1,600mg*

1. In a medium skillet, heat the oil over medium heat until it shimmers.

2. Add the onion, broccoli slaw, and turkey. Allow the turkey to brown on one side, flip, then break up into crumbles. Sprinkle in the adobo seasoning, and cook for 6 to 7 minutes, until the turkey is cooked through. Remove from the heat.

3. Meanwhile, preheat the oven to 300°F. Line a baking sheet with parchment paper.

4. Layer the tortilla chips on the prepared baking sheet. Spoon the turkey mixture on top of the chips, distributing evenly. Top with the cheese. Bake for 5 minutes, until the cheese is melted. Remove from the oven.

5. Top each serving with half of the tomatoes, lettuce, and 1 tablespoon of sour cream (if using).

USE IT UP: Adobo seasoning is also used in Pineapple Chicken (page 86). You can use up any leftover salsa or guacamole in this recipe, or create a nacho bar with your favorite ingredients, such as jalapeño, red onion, and sliced avocado.

Buffalo Turkey Meatballs

SERVES 2 / PREP TIME: 10 MINUTES / COOK TIME: 15 MINUTES

My friend Melissa inspired this recipe because she is always cooking lightened up versions of restaurant food. Enjoy the flavors of wing night at home with this version, which features meatballs. Save time by buying pre-shredded lettuce. Serve this dish over rice or in a sub roll if you want more sustenance in your meal.

Nonstick cooking spray, for coating

8 ounces ground turkey

2 tablespoons grated yellow onion

2 celery stalks, finely chopped (about 1 cup)

¼ cup crumbled blue cheese, plus 2 tablespoons for garnish (optional)

¼ cup Buffalo sauce or wing sauce

4 cups shredded lettuce

Per Serving: *Calories: 295; Fat: 18g; Carbohydrates: 7g; Fiber: 4g; Sugar: 3g; Protein: 28g; Sodium: 885mg*

1. Preheat the oven to 400°F. Line a baking sheet with aluminum foil, and spray with cooking spray.
2. In a large bowl, combine the turkey, onion, celery, and cheese. Using your hands, form 8 equal-size meatballs.
3. Put the meatballs on the baking sheet, and bake for 12 to 14 minutes, flipping halfway through, until the internal temperature reaches 165°F. Remove from the oven.
4. Allow the meatballs to cool slightly, then transfer to a medium bowl. Add the Buffalo sauce, and toss until evenly coated.
5. Divide the shredded lettuce evenly between 2 bowls. Top with the meatballs. Sprinkle each serving with 1 tablespoon of cheese (if using).

PAIRS WELL WITH: These meatballs go nicely with a side of hot rice or roasted diced potatoes.

USE IT UP: Any extra celery can be used up in Quick Beef Stew (page 130).

Rosemary Turkey Skillet

SERVES 2 / PREP TIME: 5 MINUTES / COOK TIME: 10 MINUTES

This skillet dinner is such a delicious combination of flavors and textures you'll probably forget that it's also easy. Frozen butternut squash cubes make this dish a cinch to whip up, but you can also use fresh precut butternut squash (although it may take longer to cook in the microwave).

1 (10-ounce) package frozen butternut squash cubes

1 tablespoon salted butter

1 teaspoon avocado oil

½ cup diced yellow onion

2 garlic cloves, chopped

8 ounces ground turkey

½ cup reduced-sodium turkey broth or chicken broth

¼ cup raisins

2 tablespoon fresh rosemary leaves or 1 teaspoon dried rosemary

¼ teaspoon freshly ground black pepper

Per Serving: *Calories: 418; Fat: 18g; Carbohydrates: 44g; Fiber: 5g; Sugar: 18g; Protein: 27g; Sodium: 306mg*

1. In a medium skillet, cook the butternut squash according to the package instructions. Remove from the heat. Transfer to a small bowl. Using a potato masher or fork, mash until smooth. Stir in the butter.

2. Wipe the skillet clean, then heat the oil over medium heat until it shimmers. Add the onion, garlic, and turkey. Cook, stirring frequently to break the turkey into crumbles, for 2 minutes. Add the broth, raisins, rosemary, and pepper, and stir until well combined. Cook, stirring occasionally, for another 3 to 4 minutes, until the broth has reduced by half. Remove from the heat.

3. Divide the mashed butternut squash evenly between 2 bowls, and top with the turkey mixture.

PAIRS WELL WITH: Turkey pairs well with an unoaked chardonnay with a buttery finish.

MAKE IT EASIER: If the butternut squash package includes directions for microwaving, you can take that route for even easier prep.

Cranberry-Pecan Chicken with Charred Vegetables

SERVES 2 / PREP TIME: 10 MINUTES / COOK TIME: 20 MINUTES

Many years ago I taught cooking classes with a good friend, and he showed me this method for roasting chicken. Stuffing the cranberry-pecan mixture under the skin produces a flavorful, juicy piece of chicken. Use a leave-in, oven-safe digital thermometer so you know exactly when to take out the chicken and can relax during cooking. You can easily substitute bone-in, skin-on chicken breast, but the cooking time may be longer.

2 boneless, skin-on chicken thighs

1 tablespoon butter, melted

2 tablespoons finely chopped pecans

1 tablespoon chopped unsweetened dried cranberries

¼ teaspoon dried thyme

¼ teaspoon kosher salt, plus more to season

1 tablespoon avocado oil

2 cups packed coarsely chopped kale leaves

1 cup trimmed and halved green beans

Freshly ground black pepper

1. Preheat the oven to 375°F. Line a baking sheet with parchment paper. Place the chicken thighs, skin-side up, on one side of the prepared baking sheet.

2. In a small bowl, combine the butter, pecans, cranberries, thyme, and ¼ teaspoon of salt. Stir well.

3. Using your fingers, gently loosen the skin on the chicken, being careful not to rip holes. Spoon the pecan mixture under the skin, and rub over the meat. Bake for 18 to 20 minutes, until the internal temperature reaches 160°F. Remove from the oven, and let rest for a few minutes.

Per Serving: *Calories: 625; Fat: 50g; Carbohydrates: 10g; Fiber: 3g; Sugar: 6g; Protein: 34g; Sodium: 535mg*

4. Meanwhile, in a medium skillet, heat the oil over medium-high heat until it shimmers. Add the kale and green beans. Cook, undisturbed, for 1 minute, toss, and cook, undisturbed, for another 1 minute. Toss once more, and season with a pinch each of salt and pepper. Cook for another 2 minutes undisturbed, then toss. Continue cooking for a total of 5 to 6 minutes, until the vegetables have char marks. Remove from the heat.

5. Divide the vegetables evenly between 2 plates, and serve the chicken alongside.

PAIRS WELL WITH: To make this meal a little more substantial, dice a russet potato, toss in oil, season with salt and pepper, and add it to the baking sheet with the chicken.

Chapter 6

Pork and Beef

BLTA Sushi

SERVES 2 / PREP TIME: 10 MINUTES / COOK TIME: 20 MINUTES

Homemade sushi is a fun and interactive dinner. This modern take on a BLT will certainly leave you happy and satisfied. Save even more time by prepping your rice beforehand. Rolling sushi takes a little practice, but you'll get the hang of it quickly.

½ cup sushi rice, rinsed

¾ cup water

1 tablespoon rice vinegar

4 bacon slices

2 sheets nori seaweed

2 small plum tomatoes, seeded and cut lengthwise into strips

½ medium Hass avocado, pitted, peeled, and sliced

1 cup packed shredded crispy lettuce, like iceberg or romaine

Sriracha, for serving (optional)

1. In a small pot, combine the rice and water, and bring to a boil over medium-high heat. Reduce the heat to medium-low, cover, and simmer for 15 minutes, until the rice is tender and has absorbed most of the liquid. Immediately remove the rice from the pot and spread it over a large plate or baking sheet to cool until ready to assemble. Sprinkle the cooked rice with the vinegar.

2. Meanwhile, preheat the oven to 375°F. Line a baking sheet with aluminum foil. Lay the bacon flat on the prepared baking sheet. Bake for 15 to 20 minutes, until crispy. Remove from the oven. Transfer to a paper towel–lined plate to cool. Using a knife, chop the cooled bacon into bite-size pieces.

3. Lay out 1 square foot of parchment paper on a cutting board. Place a nori sheet on the parchment paper.

4. Set up a small bowl of water. Wet your fingertips, and spread ¾ cup of the cooked rice in a thin layer on the nori sheet, leaving a ½-inch space at the top edge. Be sure to spread the rice to both sides.

Per Serving: *Calories: 369; Fat: 15g; Carbohydrates: 49g; Fiber: 5g; Sugar: 3g; Protein: 11g; Sodium: 367mg*

5. Sprinkle half of the bacon bits on top of the rice. At the bottom edge of the nori, working from left to right, place about 6 tomato slices, 3 avocado slices, and several pinches of lettuce.

6. Roll the sushi: Starting at the longest edge closest to you, lift the parchment paper, and roll the sushi onto itself one time, about halfway up. Through the parchment paper, gently squeeze the roll to tighten. Lift the parchment paper, and roll the nori again to close on itself. Gently squeeze a second time through the parchment paper to tightly seal.

7. Using a sharp knife, cut the sushi roll in half, then cut each in half again. Cut the quarters into ¼-inch-thick pieces so you end up with 8 pieces of sushi. Repeat the process with the other sheet of nori, remaining rice, bacon bits, tomato, avocado, and lettuce. Serve with a squeeze of sriracha (if using).

MAKE IT EASIER: Skip baking the bacon, and use precooked bacon or chopped beef jerky instead. Cook your rice in a rice cooker or electric pressure cooker to shorten the cook time.

Bacon, Brussels Sprouts, and Egg Bowls

SERVES 2 / PREP TIME: 5 MINUTES / COOK TIME: 25 MINUTES

"A little bacon helps the Brussels sprouts go down"—that's my slogan for this recipe. Using a small amount of a big flavor ingredient, like bacon, is a great way to make a vegetable like Brussels sprouts more enjoyable. If you want more protein, add more than one egg per person.

1 cup water

¼ cup 2 percent milk

¼ cup yellow cornmeal

⅛ teaspoon kosher salt, plus more to season (optional)

¼ cup shredded cheddar cheese

4 bacon slices

2 garlic cloves, minced

1 cup finely chopped or shaved Brussels sprouts

⅛ teaspoon smoked paprika (optional)

1 teaspoon avocado oil (optional)

2 large eggs

Freshly ground black pepper (optional)

1. In a small pot, bring the water to a boil.

2. Meanwhile, in a small bowl, whisk together the milk, cornmeal, and ⅛ teaspoon of salt. Slowly pour the mixture into the boiling water, stirring constantly. Reduce the heat to low, and cook, stirring continuously, for about 1 minute, until thickened. Cover, and cook, stirring occasionally, for another 5 minutes. Remove from the heat, fold in the cheese, and cover.

3. Heat a medium skillet over medium heat. Put the bacon in the skillet, and cook for about 6 minutes, flipping as needed, until crispy. Transfer to a paper towel–lined plate. When cool enough to handle, chop into bite-size pieces.

4. Using a paper towel, carefully wipe some of the bacon grease out of the skillet (holding the paper towel with tongs works well). Put the garlic in the skillet, and cook over medium heat for about 30 seconds, until fragrant. Add the Brussels sprouts, and cook, stirring occasionally, for 4 minutes, until tender. Transfer the Brussels sprouts to the plate with the bacon. Sprinkle with the paprika (if using).

Per Serving: *Calories: 458; Fat: 33g; Carbohydrates: 20g; Fiber: 3g; Sugar: 3g; Protein: 21g; Sodium: 942mg*

5. If the skillet is dry, add 1 teaspoon of oil. Crack the eggs into the skillet, and season with salt and pepper if desired. Fry the eggs, untouched, for 5 to 6 minutes, until the whites have set, or to your preference. Remove from the heat.

6. Meanwhile, assemble the bowls: dividing evenly, layer the cornmeal and Brussels sprouts in 2 bowls. Sprinkle with the bacon pieces. Top each with an egg. Serve immediately.

USE IT UP: The yellow cornmeal in this recipe can also be used in Cornmeal-Crusted Flounder with Zucchini (page 73) and Spicy Chicken Sandwiches (page 82). Extra bacon can be used up in BLTA Sushi (page 108).

Creamy Tomato and Kielbasa Pasta

SERVES 2 / PREP TIME: 10 MINUTES / COOK TIME: 20 MINUTES

Creamy pasta dishes are usually made with heavy cream and are therefore high in saturated fat. Swapping in fresh goat cheese still gives you an indulgent, creamy sauce and keeps the dish light. This all-in-one pasta dish delivers big flavor and is a vehicle for plenty of great vegetables.

1 cup dried high-fiber pasta

1 teaspoon avocado oil

2 garlic cloves, finely chopped or minced

1 cup grape tomatoes or cherry tomatoes, halved

6 ounces kielbasa, cut into half-moon shapes

1 teaspoon dried basil

1½ cups fresh spinach, cut into ribbons

1 cup matchstick or shredded carrots (optional)

1 ounce goat cheese

Pinch kosher salt

¼ teaspoon freshly ground black pepper

1. Bring a medium pot of water to a boil over high heat. Add the pasta, and cook to al dente according to the package instructions. Remove from the heat. Drain, reserving 1 cup of the pasta cooking water.

2. In a large skillet, heat the oil over medium heat until it shimmers. Add the garlic, and cook for 30 seconds, until fragrant.

3. Stir in the tomatoes. Increase the heat to medium-high, and continue cooking for 8 to 10 minutes, until the tomatoes are very soft and release their juices.

4. Stir in the kielbasa, and reduce the heat to medium-low. Add the basil, spinach, and carrots (if using), and stir until the spinach is wilted. Add the cheese, and stir until melted and well incorporated.

Per Serving: *Calories: 597;*
Fat 31g; Carbohydrates:
56g; Fiber: 5g; Protein: 25g;
Sodium: 873mg

5. Add the cooked pasta, and stir until well coated. Season with salt and pepper. If the sauce seems too thick, add the reserved pasta cooking water, 1 tablespoon at a time, until you achieve the desired consistency. Remove from the heat.

6. Divide the pasta evenly between 2 bowls.

USE IT UP: Save any leftover kielbasa for a super easy protein snack or speedy appetizer. Simply cut it in half lengthwise, and sear it, flat-side down, in a hot skillet for a couple of minutes. Serve with mustard for dipping.

Wild Rice and Sausage Casserole

SERVES 2 / PREP TIME: 5 MINUTES / COOK TIME: 25 MINUTES

Casseroles should be comforting, delicious, and easy. I made this version a little lighter by omitting the cream, but it still delivers plenty of flavor thanks to a touch of sausage and cream cheese.

Nonstick cooking spray, for coating the ramekins

1 (8.8-ounce) microwavable package mixed long-grain and wild rice

4 ounces sweet or hot Italian pork sausage

1 (4-ounce) can mushrooms, drained

¼ cup unsalted broth (chicken, beef, or vegetable)

1 cup finely chopped broccoli

2 tablespoons Dijon mustard

1 ounce cream cheese

Per Serving: *Calories: 418; Fat: 23g; Carbohydrates: 34g; Fiber: 5g; Sugar: 4g; Protein: 16g; Sodium: 1,175mg*

1. Preheat the oven to 400°F. Spray 2 square ramekins (about 4½ inches by 4½ inches) with cooking spray.
2. Put the rice in a large mixing bowl. Crumble in the sausage, using your fingers to break it up into small pieces. Stir in the mushrooms, broth, broccoli, and mustard.
3. Spoon the rice mixture into the prepared ramekins, filling only halfway. Working with about ½ teaspoon at a time, using a spoon, form the cream cheese into balls. Divide the cream cheese balls evenly between the ramekins. Fill to the top with the remaining rice mixture, pressing down gently using a spoon.
4. Put the ramekins on a baking sheet. Bake for 25 minutes, until the sausage is fully cooked. Remove from the oven. Let cool for about 5 minutes before serving.

PAIRS WELL WITH: Add even more vegetables to this casserole by including ½ cup grated carrots or zucchini in the rice mixture. You can also serve more vegetables on the side: try a kale salad (with kale left over from Parmesan Chicken over Wild Rice on page 92) or roasted eggplant (left over from Sheet Pan Shrimp Bowls on page 59).

Chile-Lime Pork Chops with Slaw

SERVES 2 / PREP TIME: 5 MINUTES / COOK TIME: 10 MINUTES

Boneless pork loin chops are lean and cook fast. Use ¾-inch-thick chops for this recipe; if you can only find thinner cuts, adjust the cook time as needed. This meal is high in protein and low in carbs, but you can add a side of rice or even beans if you'd like.

½ teaspoon chipotle chile powder

Juice of 1 lime

Pinch kosher salt

2 center-cut boneless pork loin chops (about ¾ inch thick)

1½ cups shredded purple cabbage

2 tablespoons red-wine vinegar

2 teaspoons avocado oil, divided

1 medium sweet apple, peeled, cored, and shredded

2 tablespoons chopped fresh cilantro leaves (optional)

Per Serving: *Calories: 410; Fat: 14g; Carbohydrates: 21g; Fiber: 4g; Sugar: 14g; Protein: 49g; Sodium: 172mg*

1. In a small bowl, combine the chipotle powder, lime juice, and salt. Brush onto the pork chops.
2. To make the slaw, in a medium mixing bowl, combine the cabbage, vinegar, 1 teaspoon of oil, and the apple. Set aside, and toss occasionally.
3. In a medium skillet, heat the remaining 1 teaspoon of oil over medium-high heat until it shimmers. Add the pork chops, and cook for about 3 minutes on each side, until the internal temperature reaches 145°F. Remove from the heat.
4. Serve the pork chops with a side of slaw. Sprinkle the slaw with the cilantro (if using).

USE IT UP: You can use any leftover cabbage in Baked Tilapia Tacos (page 66) and cilantro leaves in Banh Mi–Style Sandwiches (page 96).

Mango Salsa Pork Chops

SERVES 2 / PREP TIME: 10 MINUTES / COOK TIME: 15 MINUTES

Pork chops don't need much seasoning when topped with a tasty salsa. If you're short on time, you can use store-bought salsa.

½ cup quick-cooking white or brown rice or microwavable pouch rice

1 teaspoon avocado oil, plus 1 tablespoon

2 to 4 tablespoons minced jalapeño

¾ cup diced mango (about 1 mango)

3 tablespoons diced red onion

Juice of ½ lime

2 lean boneless pork loin chops (½ to ¾ inch thick)

Kosher salt

Freshly ground black pepper

1 (8-ounce) bag sugar snap peas

1 tablespoon minced fresh cilantro (optional)

Per Serving: *Calories: 451; Fat: 9g; Carbohydrates: 39g; Fiber: 5g; Sugar: 13g; Protein: 52g; Sodium: 148mg*

1. Prepare the rice according to the package instructions.
2. To make the mango salsa, in a medium skillet, heat 1 teaspoon of oil over medium-high heat until it shimmers. Add the jalapeño, and cook for about 2 minutes, until softened. Transfer to a bowl. Add the mango, onion, and lime juice. Stir to combine.
3. Season the pork chops on both sides with a pinch each of salt and pepper. In the same skillet, heat the remaining 1 tablespoon of oil until it shimmers. Add the pork chops, and cook for about 4 minutes on each side, until the internal temperature reaches a minimum of 145°F. Remove from the heat.
4. Meanwhile, cook the snap peas according to the package instructions.
5. Divide the snap peas evenly between 2 plates. Stir the cilantro (if using) into the cooked rice and divide the rice evenly alongside the sugar snap peas. Plate the pork chops, and top with the mango salsa.

USE IT UP: If you can't find sugar snap peas, use any leftover vegetables you have on hand. Enjoy them raw or steamed in the microwave, or stir-fry them in the skillet while the pork is cooking. You can also use up any leftover rice in this recipe.

Pork Tenderloin Medallions and Green Beans

SERVES 2 / PREP TIME: 5 MINUTES / COOK TIME: 15 MINUTES

Pork tenderloin typically takes a while to roast or slow-cook, but it's too delicious and lean not to enjoy on a busy weekend. Cutting the pork into medallions makes for a fast meal. This recipe calls for 8 ounces; if you can't find that cut, use half a full tenderloin, and freeze the rest. A quick pan sauce of wine and dried figs adds a touch of class. If you prefer a smoother sauce, use ⅓ cup fig preserves instead of dried figs. Swap out the green beans for any favorite vegetable, and add some toasty bread if you need more sustenance.

8 ounces pork tenderloin

Kosher salt

Freshly ground black pepper

1 tablespoon avocado oil

2 tablespoons diced shallots

2 garlic cloves, minced

½ cup medium-bodied red wine, like pinot noir

½ cup finely chopped dried figs

1 teaspoon balsamic vinegar

1 (8-ounce) microwavable bag fresh or frozen green beans (or about 2 cups)

¼ cup slivered almonds or chopped walnuts

1. Using a sharp knife, cut the pork tenderloin into 1-inch-thick medallions. Season both sides with a pinch each of salt and pepper.

2. In a medium skillet, heat the oil over medium-high heat until it shimmers. Add the pork, and cook for 3 to 4 minutes on each side, until the internal temperature reaches 145°F. Transfer to a plate, and tent with foil.

3. Reduce the heat to medium. Put the shallots and garlic in the same skillet. Cook for 1 minute, until fragrant. Add the wine, and using a wooden spoon, scrape up any browned bits from the bottom. Add the figs and vinegar, and simmer for 3 minutes, until the wine is reduced by half. Remove from the heat.

Per Serving: *Calories: 398; Fat: 19g; Carbohydrates: 20g; Fiber: 5g; Sugar: 11g; Protein: 28g; Sodium: 224mg*

4. Meanwhile, cook the green beans according to the package instructions. Divide evenly between 2 plates. Season with salt and pepper if desired and sprinkle with the almonds.

5. Serve the pork alongside the green beans, topped with the fig sauce.

USE IT UP: Vacuum seal and freeze the remaining half of the tenderloin for a future meal or sub it in for the pork chops in Chile-Lime Pork Chops with Slaw (page 115).

Bean and Beef Taco Bowls

SERVES 2 / PREP TIME: 10 MINUTES / COOK TIME: 15 MINUTES

This spin on the traditional taco incorporates the crunch of a tostada and provides plenty of plant protein. If desired, load up the bowls with additional toppings like shredded lettuce, sliced olives, diced avocado, sour cream, diced onions, cilantro, and salsa.

2 (10-inch) whole-wheat tortillas

4 ounces lean ground beef sirloin

2 garlic cloves, minced

1 (15.5-ounce) can pinto beans, rinsed and drained

¼ cup unsalted broth (chicken, beef, or vegetable)

¼ teaspoon ground cumin

1 plum tomato, seeded and diced

½ cup shredded cheddar jack cheese

1. Preheat the oven to 350°F.
2. In a muffin tin, gently mold the tortillas to fit into each of 2 cups, making bowls. Fold out the edges to form large rims on each bowl. Bake for 7 minutes, until crispy and lightly browned. Remove from the oven. Keep the tortilla bowls in the muffin tin, and keep the oven on.
3. Meanwhile, put the beef in a medium skillet, and cook over medium heat, stirring frequently to break it into crumbles, for 3 minutes, until browned and cooked through. Transfer to a plate.
4. Put the garlic in the same skillet, and cook, stirring constantly, for 30 seconds, until fragrant. Add the beans, broth, and cumin, and stir to combine. Simmer for 2 to 3 minutes, until the mixture has thickened. Turn off the heat. Using a potato masher, mash the beans.

Per Serving: *Calories: 479; Fat: 20g; Carbohydrates: 45g; Fiber: 12g; Sugar: 2g; Protein: 31g; Sodium: 444mg*

5. Spoon the bean mixture into the tortilla bowls, dividing evenly and pressing down gently to remove any air bubbles. Spread the beans on the rim of the tortilla, too. Sprinkle the cooked beef crumbles on top of the beans, then divide the tomato evenly between the 2 bowls. Top each with ¼ cup of cheese.

6. Bake for 5 minutes, until the cheese is melted. Remove from the oven.

7. Serve on a plate or in a shallow bowl, sprinkled with desired toppings.

MAKE IT EASIER: You can buy canned refried beans instead of making your own. Look for a vegetarian option without hydrogenated or saturated fats.

Beef Lettuce Wraps

SERVES 2 / PREP TIME: 10 MINUTES / COOK TIME: 10 MINUTES

People often think they have to choose between eating animal protein or plants, but blending the two can be a delicious, easy way to get a balanced diet. Mushrooms and eggplant add umami flavor and hearty texture to this filling.

8 ounces lean ground beef

1½ cups finely diced eggplant

1½ cups finely diced mushrooms

3 garlic cloves, finely chopped

⅓ cup unsalted beef broth

1 tablespoon hoisin sauce

¼ cup lightly salted roasted cashews, coarsely chopped

6 to 8 large iceberg or butter lettuce leaves

1 cup shredded or matchstick carrots

Pickled ginger, for garnish

Per Serving: *Calories: 318; Fat: 12g; Carbohydrates: 23g; Fiber: 5g; Sugar: 9g; Protein: 32g; Sodium: 315mg*

1. Put the beef in a medium skillet, and cook over medium heat, stirring frequently to break it into crumbles, for 3 minutes, until browned and fully cooked through. Transfer to a plate.
2. Put the eggplant in the same skillet, and cook, stirring occasionally, for 3 minutes, until softened. Add the mushrooms, garlic, and broth. Cook, stirring to scrape up any browned bits from the bottom, for another 3 minutes, until all the vegetables are tender.
3. Return the beef to the skillet. Add the hoisin sauce and cashews. Stir to combine, and remove from the heat.
4. Serve the beef mixture wrapped in the lettuce leaves, garnished with the carrots and pickled ginger.

USE IT UP: Use up any extra hoisin in Sweet Potato Hash (page 42) or Banh Mi–Style Sandwiches (page 96). Extra mushrooms can be used up in Parmesan Chicken over Wild Rice (page 92) while cashews are used again in Mango-Cashew Chicken with Sweet Peas (page 91).

Easy Meatballs over Zucchini Noodles

SERVES 2 / PREP TIME: 10 MINUTES / COOK TIME: 10 MINUTES

Meatballs are a major comfort food in my house. They take very little time to prepare and taste great over nutritious zucchini noodles, which are often found in the produce or freezer sections of your grocery store. This recipe easily doubles for bigger portions, more people, or to freeze for later.

Nonstick cooking spray, for coating

1 large egg

½ teaspoon dried oregano

⅛ teaspoon kosher salt

⅛ teaspoon freshly ground black pepper

2 tablespoons grated white onion

3 tablespoons plain or seasoned bread crumbs

8 ounces ground beef sirloin

1 (10-ounce) package frozen zucchini noodles or 1 medium zucchini, spiralized

1 cup store-bought marinara sauce

Freshly grated Parmesan cheese (optional)

Per Serving: *Calories: 374; Fat: 17g; Carbohydrates: 24g; Fiber: 5g; Sugar: 12g; Protein: 31g; Sodium: 919mg*

1. Position an oven rack about 7 inches from the broiler. Preheat the broiler to high. Line a baking sheet with aluminum foil, and lightly spray with cooking spray.

2. In a medium bowl, beat the egg. Add the oregano, salt, pepper, onion, bread crumbs, and beef. Mix well. Using your hands, form the mixture into 8 equal-size meatballs. Space them evenly apart on the prepared baking sheet.

3. Broil for 6 minutes, until the internal temperature reaches 165°F. Remove from the oven.

4. Meanwhile, cook the zucchini noodles according to the package instructions. Steam fresh zucchini noodles quickly in the microwave, or enjoy them raw.

5. Put the marinara sauce in a microwave-safe bowl, and heat in 1-minute intervals until warm. Transfer the cooked meatballs to the bowl with the sauce. Stir until well coated.

6. Divide the zucchini noodles evenly between 2 plates. Top with the meatballs and sauce. Garnish with cheese (if using).

PAIRS WELL WITH: Enjoy this meal with your favorite red wine. I recommend a full-bodied red blend.

Beef-Broccoli Stir-Fry

SERVES 2 / PREP TIME: 5 MINUTES / COOK TIME: 10 MINUTES

Broccoli slaw is a veggie hack I rely on often in my kitchen because it's so easy to add to meals. You can typically find it in the produce section with the bagged cut vegetables or in the salad section. Choose a lean ground beef like 90 percent sirloin, and add more sriracha if you prefer more heat. This recipe is naturally low in carbs.

6 ounces ground beef sirloin

½ cup diced red onion (about ¼ onion)

2 garlic cloves, minced

2 cups store-bought broccoli slaw

1½ cups frozen riced cauliflower

⅛ teaspoon freshly ground white or black pepper

1 tablespoon reduced-sodium soy sauce

½ teaspoon toasted sesame seeds

Sriracha, for serving (optional)

Per Serving: *Calories: 242; Fat: 9g; Carbohydrates: 18g; Fiber: 6g; Sugar: 7g; Protein: 24g; Sodium: 335mg*

1. Heat a dry medium skillet over medium heat. Put the beef in the skillet, and cook, stirring frequently to break it into crumbles, for 3 minutes, until completely browned. Transfer to a plate.

2. Put the onion and garlic in the same skillet, and cook, stirring frequently, for 2 minutes, until the onion has softened and garlic is fragrant. Add the broccoli slaw and cauliflower. Cook, stirring frequently, for 5 minutes.

3. Return the beef to the skillet, and stir well. Remove from the heat. Stir in the pepper and soy sauce.

4. Divide the stir-fry evenly between 2 bowls. Garnish with the sesame seeds and drizzle with the sriracha (if using).

USE IT UP: Leftover broccoli slaw can be used in Adobo Turkey Nachos (page 101).

Orange Beef and Broccoli over Rice

SERVES 2 / PREP TIME: 10 MINUTES / COOK TIME: 10 MINUTES

Sirloin cap steaks are lean, full of flavor, and affordable. If you can't find them, ask your butcher, or try one New York strip steak instead. If you like more of a kick, add more ground ginger.

FOR THE ORANGE SAUCE

½ cup orange juice

1 garlic clove, minced

½ teaspoon ground ginger

2 teaspoons rice vinegar

1½ teaspoons cornstarch

FOR THE BEEF, BROCCOLI, AND RICE

1 (6-ounce) beef sirloin cap steak

Kosher salt

Freshly ground black pepper

1 tablespoon avocado oil

2 cups frozen broccoli florets

1 (8.8-ounce) pouch microwavable brown rice

Per Serving: *Calories: 381; Fat: 13g; Carbohydrates: 45g; Fiber: 5g; Sugar: 7g; Protein: 24g; Sodium: 154mg*

1. **MAKE THE ORANGE SAUCE:** In a small bowl, whisk together the orange juice, garlic, ginger, vinegar, and cornstarch.
2. **MAKE THE BEEF, BROCCOLI, AND RICE:** Using a sharp knife, cut the beef into very thin strips, 1 to 2 inches long. Season with a pinch each of salt and pepper.
3. In a medium skillet, heat the oil over medium-high heat until it shimmers. Add the beef, and cook for 1 to 2 minutes, until a small amount of redness remains. Transfer to a plate.
4. To the same skillet, add the broccoli, and cook for 3 to 4 minutes, until crisp-tender. Add the orange sauce, and cook for about 2 minutes, until it starts to thicken. Reduce the heat to low, and keep warm.
5. Meanwhile, prepare the rice according to the package instructions.
6. Return the beef to the skillet, and toss in the sauce until well coated. Remove from the heat.
7. Divide the rice evenly between 2 bowls. Top with the orange beef and broccoli.

PAIRS WELL WITH: You can add any vegetables to this recipe, including cauliflower, snap peas, carrots, or zucchini.

Strawberry and Flank Steak Quinoa Bowls

SERVES 2 / PREP TIME: 15 MINUTES / COOK TIME: 15 MINUTES

Strawberries and steak is one of my favorite under-the-radar flavor combinations. Roasted strawberries produce a delicious all-natural sauce that makes the steak taste incredible. Ask your butcher to slice a flank steak in thirds so you have a perfect 6- to 8-ounce portion. Vacuum seal and freeze the rest, and use it as a substitute in Steak and Mashed Potatoes (page 128). You can up the vegetables in this dish by roasting a bag of mixed vegetables on a lower rack in the oven while broiling the meat.

½ cup quinoa, rinsed and drained

1 cup water

3 cups packed chopped spinach leaves

1 (8-ounce) package strawberries, halved lengthwise

1 (6- to 8-ounce) beef flank steak

1 teaspoon extra-virgin olive oil

½ teaspoon kosher salt

½ teaspoon freshly ground black pepper

¼ cup crumbled goat cheese

¼ cup chopped walnuts

1. In a small pot, combine the quinoa and water, and bring to a boil over medium-high heat. Reduce the heat to low, cover, and simmer for 15 minutes, until the quinoa is tender and has absorbed most of the liquid. Remove from the heat. Stir in the spinach, and cover.

2. Meanwhile, position an oven rack 3 to 4 inches from the broiler. Preheat the broiler to high.

3. Line a baking sheet with aluminum foil. Use an additional piece of foil to make a basket about half the size of the pan by folding up the edges 1 to 2 inches. Put the strawberries in the foil basket, and place on one side of the baking sheet.

Per Serving: *Calories: 486; Fat: 22g; Carbohydrates: 43g; Fiber: 8g; Sugar: 8g; Protein: 31g; Sodium: 731mg*

4. Rub the steak with the oil, and season with the salt and pepper. Place the steak on the other side of the baking sheet. Broil for about 8 minutes, turning halfway through, until the internal temperature reaches 145°F. Remove from the oven, and let rest for 5 minutes. Using a sharp knife, cut the steak against the grain into thin strips.

5. Dividing evenly, layer the quinoa, steak, and strawberries in 2 bowls. Top each with 2 tablespoons of cheese and 2 tablespoons of walnuts.

PAIRS WELL WITH: Enjoy a fruity red wine with this meal, like an old-vine zinfandel or fruity red blend.

Steak and Mashed Potatoes

SERVES 2 / PREP TIME: 10 MINUTES / COOK TIME: 15 MINUTES

A delicious steak dinner is only minutes away! If you can't find top sirloin at the store, talk to your butcher about another lean choice. The milk can be omitted from the mashed potatoes if you don't have any in the house. Serve with red wine and bread for a fancy evening in.

1 large russet potato, peeled and finely diced

1 pint cherry tomatoes

1 tablespoon balsamic vinegar, plus 1 teaspoon

1 tablespoon extra-virgin olive oil, plus 1 teaspoon

½ teaspoon kosher salt, divided

½ teaspoon freshly ground black pepper, divided

1 beef top sirloin boneless steak, cut into 2 (4- to 6-ounce) portions

1 tablespoon unsalted butter

1 tablespoon 2 percent milk

1. Put the potatoes in a small pot, and add just enough water to fully cover. Bring to a boil over high heat. Cook for about 15 minutes, until the potatoes can be easily pierced with a fork. Remove from the heat.

2. Meanwhile, position an oven rack 3 to 4 inches from the broiler. Preheat the broiler to high. Line a rimmed baking sheet with aluminum foil.

3. Using an additional piece of foil, about 1 square foot, form a square bowl by folding up the edges about 1 inch all the way around. Put the tomatoes in the aluminum foil bowl, and place on one side of the prepared baking sheet. Drizzle the tomatoes with 1 tablespoon of vinegar and 1 tablespoon of oil. Mix well.

4. To make the balsamic marinade, in a small bowl, combine the remaining 1 teaspoon of vinegar, the remaining 1 teaspoon of oil, ¼ teaspoon of salt, and ¼ teaspoon of pepper.

5. Place the steak on the other side of the baking sheet. Pour the balsamic marinade over the steak, and rub to distribute evenly.

6. Broil for 6 to 7 minutes, until the internal temperature reaches 145°F for medium-rare (or to desired doneness). Remove from the oven, and let rest for 3 to 5 minutes.

Per Serving: *Calories: 462; Fat: 20g; Carbohydrates: 41g; Fiber: 4g; Sugar: 7g; Protein: 31g; Sodium: 668mg*

7. Meanwhile, drain the potatoes, and return them to the same pot. While hot, stir to remove any excess water. Add the butter, milk, remaining ¼ teaspoon of salt, and ¼ teaspoon of pepper. Using a potato masher, mash to your desired consistency.

8. Divide the steak, tomatoes, and mashed potatoes evenly between 2 plates.

SWAP OR SUBSTITUTE: One New York strip steak cut into 2 pieces also works well here. The cooking time should be the same, although a thicker steak will take longer.

Quick Beef Stew

SERVES 2 / PREP TIME: 10 MINUTES / COOK TIME: 35 MINUTES

There's nothing more comforting on a cold evening than a bowl of beef stew, but it typically takes hours to simmer to perfection. This quick version sears in the flavor on a more tender, lean cut of beef and adds lots of vegetables.

1 tablespoon avocado oil

2 beef sirloin tip steaks, cut into ½-inch dice

Kosher salt

Freshly ground black pepper

¼ cup full-bodied red wine, like cabernet sauvignon

3 cups unsalted beef broth

2 carrots, sliced (about 1 cup)

2 celery stalks, cut into ¼-inch pieces (about 1 cup)

1 medium russet potato, peeled and diced (about 1 cup)

¼ cup diced onion

1 tablespoon tomato paste

¼ teaspoon dried thyme

Per Serving: *Calories: 442; Fat: 21g; Carbohydrates: 31g; Fiber: 5g; Sugar: 7g; Protein: 33g; Sodium: 971mg*

1. In a medium Dutch oven, heat the oil over medium heat until it shimmers.
2. Season the beef with a pinch each of salt and pepper. Add to the pot, and cook for 1 minute on each side. Stir in the wine, and simmer, stirring with a wooden spoon to pick up any browned bits at the bottom, for 1 minute.
3. Add the broth, carrots, celery, potatoes, onion, tomato paste, and thyme. Increase the heat to high, and bring the mixture to a boil. Reduce the heat, cover, and simmer for 25 minutes, until the vegetables are tender and the stew has thickened. Remove from the heat.
4. Divide the stew evenly between 2 bowls.

USE IT UP: Don't feel restricted in the quantities of vegetables. Load up with as much as you like, or add other vegetables like mushrooms or parsnips. Enjoy a glass of the cabernet you used in the recipe alongside your meal.

Measurement Conversions

VOLUME EQUIVALENTS	U.S. STANDARD	U.S. STANDARD (OUNCES)	METRIC (APPROXIMATE)
LIQUID	2 tablespoons	1 fl. oz.	30 mL
	¼ cup	2 fl. oz.	60 mL
	½ cup	4 fl. oz.	120 mL
	1 cup	8 fl. oz.	240 mL
	1½ cups	12 fl. oz.	355 mL
	2 cups or 1 pint	16 fl. oz.	475 mL
	4 cups or 1 quart	32 fl. oz.	1 L
	1 gallon	128 fl. oz.	4 L
DRY	⅛ teaspoon	–	0.5 mL
	¼ teaspoon	–	1 mL
	½ teaspoon	–	2 mL
	¾ teaspoon	–	4 mL
	1 teaspoon	–	5 mL
	1 tablespoon	–	15 mL
	¼ cup	–	59 mL
	⅓ cup	–	79 mL
	½ cup	–	118 mL
	⅔ cup	–	156 mL
	¾ cup	–	177 mL
	1 cup	–	235 mL
	2 cups or 1 pint	–	475 mL
	3 cups	–	700 mL
	4 cups or 1 quart	–	1 L
	½ gallon	–	2 L
	1 gallon	–	4 L

OVEN TEMPERATURES

FAHRENHEIT	CELSIUS (APPROXIMATE)
250°F	120°C
300°F	150°C
325°F	165°C
350°F	180°C
375°F	190°C
400°F	200°C
425°F	220°C
450°F	230°C

WEIGHT EQUIVALENTS

U.S. STANDARD	METRIC (APPROXIMATE)
½ ounce	15 g
1 ounce	30 g
2 ounces	60 g
4 ounces	115 g
8 ounces	225 g
12 ounces	340 g
16 ounces or 1 pound	455 g

Index

About the Author

Jenna Braddock is a Registered Dietitian Nutritionist, Certified Specialist in Sports Dietetics, and ACSM Certified Personal Trainer living in St. Augustine, Florida, with her husband, Brian, and two sons. Jenna's mission is to "Make Healthy Easy" so you have more space to live vibrantly and love others well. She specializes in behavior change counseling, performance nutrition, the Enneagram and eating, recipe development, and enjoyable fitness. She has had the honor of working with individuals, groups, and companies to promote realistic, balanced health strategies in addition to appearing regularly on TV and digital media outlets.

To connect with Jenna, find her on Instagram at @Make.Healthy.Easy or on her website at JennaBraddock.com.

Acknowledgments

I am blessed beyond measure by the following people:

The Registered Dietitian Nutritionists who came before and paved the way for me to write a cookbook like this.

Kerri, Cindy, Sarah Jane, Carlene, Holley, Liz, Kara, Kristina, Dr. Rodriguez, Dr. Christie, Lauri, "the Jens," Tim (and more)—my mentors and close friends I've had throughout my career. I would not be who I am without you.

The many friends who tested recipes for this book. I am touched by your willingness to participate in this project, and your feedback made every recipe better.

Mom and Dad: Thank you for believing in me every second of my life and loving me through thick and thin. Mom, thanks for instilling in me a love of cooking and being a stellar recipe tester.

Jackson and Benny: Investing in your lives is my greatest privilege. I am so thankful I get to be your mommy and for your patience in testing many, many recipes for this book. I love and treasure you both.

Brian: Being your partner is a joy and honor. I'm so grateful for your steadiness, wisdom, loyalty, and love. Thank you for believing in me and all my crazy dreams. I love you, and the COO chair will always be open for you.

Thank you, God, for Jesus and for using this jar of clay (1 Corinthians 4:5–7).

CPSIA information can be obtained
at www.ICGtesting.com
Printed in the USA
JSHW051348020321
12185JS00007B/45